How to Write a Business Plan

Win backing and support for your ideas and ventures

Brian Finch

KoganPage

First published in Great Britain and the United States in 2001 by Kogan Page Limited
Sixth edition 2019

2nd Floor, 45 Gee Street	122 W 27th St, 10th Floor	4737/23 Ansari Road
London	New York, NY 10001	Daryaganj
EC1V 3RS	USA	New Delhi 110002
United Kingdom		India
www.koganpage.com		

© Brian Finch, 2001, 2006, 2010, 2013, 2016, 2019

The right of Brian Finch to be identified as the author of this work has been asserted by him in accordance with the Copyright, Designs and Patents Act 1988.

ISBNs

Hardback	978 1 78966 002 9
Paperback	978 0 7494 8643 3
Ebook	978 0 7494 8644 0

British Library Cataloguing-in-Publication Data

A CIP record for this book is available from the British Library.

Library of Congress Cataloging-in-Publication Control Number

Names: Finch, Brian, author.
Title: How to write a business plan : win backing and support for your ideas and ventures / Brian Finch.
Description: Sixth edition. | London ; New York : Kogan Page, [2019] | Series: Creating success.
Identifiers: LCCN 2019005207 (print) | LCCN 2019008788 (ebook) | ISBN 9780749486440 (Ebook) | ISBN 9780749486433 (pbk.) | ISBN 9781789660029 (hardback)
Subjects: LCSH: Business planning. | Business writing. | New business enterprises–Planning. | Small business–Planning.
Classification: LCC HD30.28 (ebook) | LCC HD30.28 .F562 2019 (print) | DDC 658.4/012–dc23
LC record available at https://lccn.loc.gov/2019005207

Typeset by Hong Kong FIVE Workshop
Print production managed by Jellyfish
Printed and bound by CPI Group (UK) Ltd, Croydon CR0 4YY

Take your learning further with this book's online course.

All the titles in Kogan Page's Creating Success series have individual *CPD-accredited* online courses to help you develop your business and workplace skills.

Quick and easy-to-use: 1-hour courses to develop your skills quickly

CPD accreditation: Each course awards CPD points and certification for tangible proof of your achievement

Additional resources: Downloadable resources will reinforce what you learn

Bespoke packages: Discounted corporate and bespoke offers are also available

Free preview: Module preview to confirm you are picking the right one

Find out more about the course for this book at
koganpageonline.com

Save 25%
on all courses using the code CREATINGSUCCESS

04595641

CREATING SUCCESS
SERIES

The above titles are available from all good bookshops.

For further information on these and other Kogan Page titles, or to order online, visit **www.koganpage.com**.

CONTENTS

Introduction

Why this book?

You want this book because it will help you tell your story to persuade someone who will work with you to realize your vision. A template downloaded from the internet will not do that. Many of those are very good and cover most of the issues but they do it like a robot, giving you spaces to fill in with information and that often gets in the way of telling a story. It is the difference between painting by numbers and creating your own picture.

This book is designed to lead you through writing your own business plan. While there may be some elements of the finished document that will benefit from professional input from an accountant, marketing expert, etc, you should write the main elements of this plan yourself. There are two reasons for this:

- You must be able to present it in person, which is more difficult if you have not been closely involved in preparing it.

- Writing the plan helps you perfect its content.

Sitting in front of a business partner or prospective investor is a bad time to find you are not utterly familiar with the plan or that there is a hole in the logic you hadn't thought of.

I am often approached by people who want help with the actual writing of the business plan. They may not be confident in their ability to write well and it is good to get help; but the owner of the plan, the person who must sell it and carry it out, really needs to have contributed significantly to the plan.

An example of the wrong way to use an adviser was an approach I received some years ago. I talked about the business with the entrepreneur but was horrified to find only the bare outline of an idea; whenever I asked for details it was clear he did not know. That can be OK: some people are good at producing powerful visions but delegate the detail and can still be very successful. They need a committed partner to work out those details, not a professional adviser working for a daily fee. Details matter: the vision is not enough. A great idea that does not actually work is of no use at all.

What are my credentials to advise you? I have written plans to raise money from banks, venture capitalists and private investors, have been a company director, have sat where you sit; but, more importantly, I have worked in venture capital and evaluated plans like the one you are about to write and have decided whether to invest.

I started writing these books more than 25 years ago because I saw so many plans that needed help: some were not going to raise money but some were not going to work as businesses.

You will notice, as we go through this book, that there are more points to think about and everything gets more complicated. Some people will tell you that a business plan can be encapsulated in three sentences or must be capable of explanation to a six-year-old – great sentiments, just not true!

What about a one-page proposal for a great new online idea where you don't yet know how you will make money? Fortunes have been made on such proposals – and fortunes have been lost too. Three answers:

- It may work for you, but I wouldn't bet on it.
- That one-page proposal is probably the summary of a 100-page plan.
- That one page may simulate interest but the real business plan is needed to take it forward.

This book is structured to lead you through the elements that make up the typical business plan, in the order that they are likely to appear in your plan. As well as the short examples that appear within this book, you can also find extended examples online at www.koganpage.com/businessplan; but do note these are meant for guidance and not necessarily as a template to be followed in minute detail. Your business, your environment and your needs may be different from those that lie behind my 'standard model' or my illustrations; that's fine, just adapt my approach and set down your plan differently.

What is the plan for and who is the audience?

Before beginning to write, identify who the audience is and what you want their response to be.

Exercise

- Write down a definition of your purpose.
- Describe the people you will give the plan to and list what issues you need to cover for them. When you are writing your plan, you can use this as a checklist.
- Write down the range of possible responses and which one you want.
- List in two columns on a single sheet of paper why they might say yes and why they might say no.

Do you want the reader:

- to invest in your new idea or in an existing business?
- to buy your business?

- to enter a joint venture?
- to accept your tender to carry out a contract?
- to give you a grant or a regulatory approval?
- to persuade the board to change the direction of your business?

If you are looking for investment, you will concentrate on the excellent returns you will provide at low risk. However, if you are seeking approval from a parent company, you will devote more attention to strategic issues and to what other approvals and inputs you may require.

If you are trying to raise money, you will explain how good your management is, while if you are hoping to sell out and retire to the beach, you won't make yourself sound indispensable. For example, when trying to attract a buyer you will emphasize:

- the strength of your management team;
- how profitable the business is;
- what good prospects it has for future growth;
- how well it fits with the prospective purchaser's business.

If you want grants from a regulatory authority then there is extra research to carry out: the authority may give guidance setting out its objectives for investment. Get a copy of these, check that you are eligible and tick off the points that must be satisfied against your plan. They will want to be sure your project is viable but they will also look at issues such as job creation and local social benefits. They will probably want to be sure that you could not get funding by conventional means.

Maybe you are writing the plan to help you to run your own business. In that case, is the specific purpose: to help focus your ideas, to bring in ideas from others, to ensure everyone in the team is committed to the same ends or to communicate the plan to the organization? You will concentrate more on non-financial targets such as management issues, personnel development, etc. You will identify objectives for the business as a whole and, for departments, devote more detail to how these larger objectives will be met.

The response you want should also be in the front of your mind when you write the plan because it will influence what you write. If you want a response from your team, then the style will be different from merely communicating what is going to happen. If you want a potential joint venture partner to sign up, then you will stress the benefits they will get and you will ask for the deal, but more of that later.

Once you have decided who your audience is you need to write with them in mind, using language that is appropriate to them.

'I read a proposal from some academics working at a research institute. The biggest problem I had was that I couldn't understand the jargon – I still don't know what their work was all about. Even if it was a good idea, they obviously couldn't communicate with the real world.'

(Corporate financier)

This is an extreme example but the lesson is still important. Financiers like concise and clear documents with jargon clearly explained; prospective technical partners, on the other hand, need to see the technical detail; government departments need to know more about non-financial community benefits. In each case the slant of the writing will be different.

Don't try to make the same plan give different messages for completely different audiences. Make amendments to ensure there is a clear fit. However, do not write completely different plans for different audiences. First, it is an enormous amount of work, and second, different parties might meet and compare inconsistencies between their versions.

The first impression

You get one chance to make a good first impression. Grab that chance. Present a document that:

- is persuasive;
- looks good;

- is free of spelling, grammatical and numerical errors;
- covers the key issues;
- contains the necessary supporting information.

This is not to say that if you are turned down the first time, you may not try again, but it will be harder.

Imagine someone coming in to see you with a business proposal. They enter your office full of enthusiasm and dynamism. They have a brief but fluent and persuasive presentation that seems to cover all the issues and to be backed by facts. You feel good about them and about the proposal.

Now imagine the opposite. The person enters your office looking scruffy, stumbles and hesitates throughout a dull, overlong presentation, makes mistakes and does not have answers to important questions. Even if they come back after polishing the proposal you will be more reluctant to see them a second time and you will have the memory of the first fiasco.

The person you are presenting your plan to is just like you – they like a good first impression. Research tells us that we form an impression of people we meet within about 15 seconds. This is a case where the surface impression is very important. Having a sound proposal is great but first make a good impression and then you get the chance to demonstrate how good the proposal is.

This is the reason why, as dealt with later, the summary is so important. That is the make or break element of your plan.

You are telling a story

You have captured your reader's attention, now you must keep it. You must also stimulate their enthusiasm for your project so that they will back you. The story of you, your business and what you propose to do with it is a fascinating story: tell it that way. It is an exciting story of good ideas and hard work leading to success. It has a beginning, a middle and an end:

- The beginning sets the scene for the plan, it tells the background to your business and how you got here, outlining the business, management, market, etc.

- The middle explains what is special about your ideas and sets out the proposal itself.

- The end asks for what you need to carry out the plan, points to the risks but explains how they will be dealt with and highlights the rewards.

A story grabs the attention of the reader and stimulates interest and imagination. It flows... so should a business plan.

If a plan is disjointed and hard to follow, then, like a story of the same kind, it will lose the reader. To continue the comparison; you are not trying to write a great literary novel, which few people start to read and fewer finish; you are trying to write a popular novel (but not quite so long). *There is no ideal length.* It all depends on the business. A small business can still be complicated and need a lot of explaining, while a large business can be comparatively simple. Just remember to be as brief as you can. Follow the rule of getting someone you know and who will be honest with you to read your plan: ideally they should know nothing about your business or the market. After reading your plan, do they understand the key issues and are they excited by your proposals?

As with a book, it is important to remember the plot, the descriptive bits (background or scene setting) and the characters. Your plans and background are essential but so are the people who will carry it all out. Some people get the balance wrong and write endlessly about the market or about themselves or about the history of the business. Remember to balance your story and *don't bore your reader.*

Use action words

This is an adventure story, not a travelogue: use action words as much as possible. These say what you will do and when, rather than describing scenery. Use the active rather than the passive voice.

For example, 'By year three of the plan we will have expanded to 20 outlets in five countries', rather than, 'By year three of the plan the business will have 20 outlets in five countries.' Always focus on who (eg you) will do what, when and how.

It may be necessary to describe things at times but remember that brevity and actions come over more powerfully and persuasively in a business plan.

Summary

- Write briefly and keep to the point; avoid repetition.

- Focus on the key points that really matter.

- Use action words; these are much more powerful and persuasive. They convey an impression of purpose and confidence.

- Don't bore the reader.

Presentation

What about presenting online? I can see no reason not to, but all the advice here still holds except that being brief is even more important. If an investor hesitates to read a 20-page document, then online your limit is 10 pages or fewer, and diagrams and pictures are more important.

Presentation isn't everything but it is still important. While an investor may not invest in a beautiful document, they are very unlikely to back something that is scrappy and badly written. That suggests the plan has not been thought through and it is likely to end up in the bin.

Research into crowdfunding shows that a plan with a spelling error is 13 per cent less likely to be successful.

Give your proposal the best chance. Go that extra mile. You have invested time and money, hopes and emotion in the project, put in that little extra effort:

- Type the plan; don't hand anybody something that is handwritten.
- Use decent quality paper.
- Include a title page cover.
- Number the pages, and if the plan is more than three or four pages long, put in a contents page that links correctly to numbered pages.
- Don't go over the top and use lots of different fonts and colours. That makes it look desperate.
- Set out the document so that it is easy to read; put in headings, put detail in appendices, use a clear typeface (not a tiny print that the reader has to strain to read), space paragraphs out.
- If you can show diagrams or photographs of important products, premises, processes, etc, they will bring the subject alive for the reader.
- If you have a website, show screenshots of it.
- Check for spelling and grammatical errors.
- Check for numerical errors.
- Make sure all page references are correct.
- Date the document to avoid confusion with earlier or later drafts.
- Get the plan bound; it does not cost much and makes a big difference.

Some people like to number each paragraph for easy reference. Some like to have a hierarchy of headings. For example:

MAIN HEADING
Sub-heading
Sub-sub-heading

The key thing is to make the presentation clear. At the same time, don't put all your energy into producing a beautiful document that contains lots of logical flaws and does not convince.

Facts and evidence

Someone who reads a business plan is looking for confirmation, seeking evidence to persuade them that what they are reading is true. This should be provided by putting verifiable facts in the text wherever possible. These facts should be supported by numbers to set in context how relevant the fact is and to support the projections later in the report. *Provide evidence for what you say.*

'Start-ups are always hard to back. One reason is the limited evidence that is available to back the claims.

One team that approached me for finance told me about the enormous opportunity they saw to open many outlets for their business in the UK. One of the group already owned a chain of three. But amazingly he had no evidence in the document to support his estimate of the number of outlets proposed in the new business. Nor data from his own existing business to support the sales assumptions. Nor had he conducted a survey of other similar businesses to support the sales assumptions. I had to rely on his word, which he repeated frequently... but really I felt that wasn't enough to persuade me to put cash into his business.'

(Venture capitalist)

This is a real problem with people setting up new businesses. I know it can be hard getting reliable data. One client of mine trades in sugar factory equipment worldwide. When he was setting up a new venture he found it very hard to provide any figures to support his claims of market size, growth, competitors' pricing. He knew that what he was saying was true because of his years of experience but data is simply not easily available from international bodies on this international market, while local markets are often in poor countries that do not keep or publish such data. He also found it hard to forecast when sales would be achieved within the first year of trading and where they would come from. One solution is to ask your customers.

I said it is hard but look at it from the point of view of the financier, the bank or the investor; if you cannot convince them that what you are saying is right then they are not going to invest. Just telling them what you believe will not convince them: they need some evidence. It is a famous dictum of propaganda that a lie, if repeated frequently enough, becomes accepted as the truth eventually. It does not work in business plans or when trying to raise money from banks and investors. Constant repetition focuses the reader's attention on the issue and if the reader does not believe an assertion, repetition simply reinforces a climate of doubt and disbelief. *Give the facts to support your claims: don't simply repeat the claims.*

Some people, confronting this problem of persuading the reader, simply waffle. Don't waffle! It is common to read reports that go on at length about the market, the opportunity, the history of the project, and so on, but without any evidence. The plan may be badly or beautifully written but the attention of the business partner or divisional chief executive or financier was lost at the beginning, when they got bored and decided they didn't believe the hype.

For example:

Not...

This gigantic market is growing rapidly and will soon be absolutely vast, and once we have conquered it in a couple of years' time we will start on the even more ginormous European market where there is even more potential and no competition – and in any case nobody can copy our unique product.

But...

The UK market is estimated to be worth approximately 220 million per annum and to be growing at about 17 per cent per annum (*Financial Times* Survey, 28 February 2016). If development follows the course of the USA, the potential market size is about 450 million, which gives considerable room for continued growth. Trade sources (see Appendix I) suggest that the current suppliers are finding difficulty meeting demand and backlogs have grown to 18 weeks or more. This supports our sales forecasts.

We believe there are further opportunities for expansion in the European Union, where the market is at a similar stage of development to the UK four years ago. Our plans show a modest entry into the German market in 18 months...

Our product has minor improvements compared with competitors (see Appendix II), and they are protected by copyright that has been registered throughout the EU.

Most banks and venture capitalists will seek confirmation of sales forecasts, either from past trading or from speaking to prospective customers. Be ready for this and provide as much supporting information as possible: market research data, published information, extracts from management accounts, customer lists, etc.

Gathering data

Where do you get this data to support your plan? Start by recognizing the odd idea that the data does not have to be right to be included: it just needs to convince the reader. I am not saying that you should make up proof. *You should not lie.* However, you can get information from lots of sources and interpret it to suit what you honestly believe to be true.

The list below suggests some places where you can get data, in descending order of reliability:

- government statistics;
- market research reports;
- university departments;
- trade associations;

- trade press;

- newspaper articles;

- competitors' brochures and websites;

- interviews/comments from suppliers, customers and competitors;

- the World Wide Web.

Government and international trade body data are the best evidence. Such data can be tracked down by contacting industry ministries, for example.

Many (slightly out of date) market research reports are available in university libraries or specialist public libraries free of charge. In the UK, members of the public can use libraries such as the City Business Library in London to carry out research. Some university libraries will permit access from people who are not students, by arrangement.

University departments often have experts on your particular industry. Track them down and ask them what information is available and where. They may be able to refer you to published papers, but even if you just quote their views (give details of who they are), then that is some reassurance for the reader of your plan. Remember that the reader of your plan may telephone the same source you have quoted, so don't write anything that is not strictly true.

Staff at trade associations will often be very helpful. There are often both national and international associations to try. They frequently have libraries, will know who is researching particular fields and, as with academics, may be quoted in your plan. For example, if they say a market is growing at 5 per cent per annum, then you can write that, remembering to say where you got the information.

The trade press is often useful. You can telephone the journalists, who are often very knowledgeable and will also have ideas of who else you can speak to.

Press cuttings can be accessed through the libraries mentioned above and also through the internet. There may be a cost to this.

Try the trade press first but the national press is worth a go too, usually the more serious newspapers and magazines. You may find a journalist who has gathered lots of information for an article and they may share some of this with you.

The published material, including published reports and accounts, of your competitors, suppliers and customers may provide useful data. You can also try interviewing suppliers, customers and competitors. What they say must be used carefully because it may be unreliable, but sometimes it can be helpful.

Whenever you gather information by talking to people, ask them who else you can speak to. In this way you may find the recommendation of a recommendation gets you to the person who gives you a really useful fact.

Finally, remember to try searching the internet for data. There are millions of pages of information available on the internet, giving you access to universities, trade associations, government bodies, newspapers, research organizations, libraries and even amateur enthusiasts. Whilst searching can be very time-consuming, it is often worth it. If you don't find what you want immediately, then use every search engine you can: each one covers only a fraction of what is out there, so if one has nothing then another may have just the link you are looking for.

If you are using Google don't forget to use their search engine options for academic articles and also for blogs, which may lead you to information or to new sources. Always bear in mind when using the internet that ideally you want original data, not someone quoting someone quoting someone… and just because a fact is on Wikipedia does not make it right. The problem with data from the internet is that the reader of your plan can also easily check it.

If you are still stuck, think laterally; try encyclopedias, universities around the world, the Library of Congress, the British Library. Don't be afraid to email people you come across on the web to ask them if they know of any sources you can try for information.

Repetition

There is bound to be some repetition in your business plan, just as there is in this book. You need to ensure that each section of your document tells a self-contained story because a reader may read that section, put down the document and then read another section at another time. Like a novel, there may well be times when recapitulation is necessary. At the very least, your summary is meant to be a condensation of what you have said in the body of your document. You are likely to say things in your section on the business background that are mirrored in, say, the section on markets. There is nothing wrong with some repetition, indeed it reinforces and adds weight to your argument. However, you must avoid excess, particularly within the same section, because it makes your story boring and leaves a bad impression of vagueness with the reader.

Review your document

Get someone else whom you trust, but is not involved in the project, to read the document and give you feedback. You are not asking for criticism but you are asking for a constructive approach; for ideas, concerns and flaws. Don't ask for advice from a nitpicker or someone who has no business experience because they will find lots of little flaws that don't really matter much whilst missing the big logical gap that you need help on. You need someone who will be honest with you.

Summary points

- Focus the plan on what it is for and who the audience is.
- Ensure it is well presented and tells your story well, to make a good impression.
- Use facts and evidence to support your case.

01
The structure of the plan

Organize what ought to be in the plan before you start writing it. This will save you a lot of editing later on as you realize that you have put something in the wrong logical place or the wrong place for the flow of your narrative.

Exercise

You have an idea. Write a list of its key points in note form.

- What is the product or service?
- How is it different?
- What is the competition and why are you better?
- Who are the customers, how will you reach them and why will they buy?
- What will they pay?
- How will you make the product/deliver the service?
- Income and costs?
- What do you need?

Write down the key headings – leaving plenty of space between the headings – and then jot down a list of the key issues that should be in the section. These may become sub-headings in your plan but they don't have to.

For example, we wanted to establish a new chain of bookshops in the UK so we might have had the following first list of headings for key issues:

- the market background;
- why we are different;
- the management team;
- operational details;
- the proposals;
- forecasts;
- exit strategy.

This was an existing and a mature market: one that the potential readers of our business plan would think they knew well because they would be users of bookshops. Clearly we needed to explain how the market operated, in order to correct any misconceptions. Then we needed to convince them that we could make a successful new entry into this well-established marketplace with something different. In order to complete this it was essential to explain why we were a particularly strong management team and also to explain how the 'mechanics' of the trade worked, since this was where we proposed to introduce innovations. From there the issues to be covered followed a fairly standard pattern, covering the proposal itself, what we hoped to achieve (the forecasts) and how investors would get their return (exit strategy).

Within the operational details section, for example, our sub-headings were:

- customers;
- products;
- the supply chain;
- systems.

We had to explain who our customers were – and were not – in order to persuade the reader why we would get more customers than our competitors.

Under the product sub-heading we covered our product range: the most popular general books (ie not academic books), and a complementary range of CD ROMs, music CDs, greetings cards, gift wrap, etc.

The supply chain was important, again because we were intending to approach it slightly differently from our competitors, so that too had to be explained.

Finally, within this section, our systems were crucial to making our ideas work and so they needed to be discussed and explained. It was particularly important to persuade the reader that effective systems could be put in place quickly and cheaply.

Once you have produced your complete list, look at it critically. Is there anything important that is missing? Add it in – ensure that every issue that you think is important has been covered within the plan.

The exact items in a structure plan will vary from business to business but, broadly, they will be:

- summary;
- introduction;
- business background;
- the product;
- the market;
- operations;
- management;
- proposal;
- financial background:
  - trading to date;
  - forecasts;
- risks;
- conclusion;
- appendices.

The order will depend upon how it projects the story best. Remember that you are trying to tell a clear and convincing story. You may merge some sections, such as the product and the market, but on the other hand you may have extra sections that are not mentioned above.

To keep a clear structure you will find yourself repeating some things. The contents of your summary will obviously be repeated in more detail in the body of the plan. You may find some things set out in the introduction or background being repeated elsewhere. That is fine as long as you don't explain all the detail in two or three places, which will make your document boring to read.

There may be other items that are necessary to explain your business. The list above does not include anything on technology, politics, trading partners or options (concerning the different ways you may develop the business), any of which may be appropriate for particular activities.

Most businesses nowadays make extensive use of computers and the internet and so a section on technology is becoming usual. This is not a question of going into technical detail but of explaining how business critical issues have been covered. An example would be a business trading through its own website whose plan should cover who will build, maintain and host the site – giving evidence of sufficient bandwidth to support the forecasts included in the plan. This might fall within a section on operations, but depending upon how central it is to the business may justify a dedicated section.

Using appendices

Your plan may have a lot of detailed evidence to support it. If that is the case then consider carefully whether you need it to be included or whether you could just refer to it and have it ready if asked for. If you feel it adds significantly to your credibility then put it in appendices and summarize it in the plan. Always refer clearly in your plan to the appropriate appendix so that the reader can find it easily. The appendices may be in a separate bound document if that prevents the main document from being too bulky. A huge tome can be very intimidating to your reader, so try to keep the plan itself to a manageable size. It is better for the appendices to be a bulky document and for the plan to be relatively short.

Do not put detailed data or evidence in the plan itself. That disrupts the story you are telling and makes the document dull. Summarize and explain what the evidence says and refer to it. An easy example would be where you have several years of accounts for a business. It is easy to summarize the key numbers in the plan while putting the accounts themselves in a separate document.

There are two types of document you may want to put in an appendix to a plan: 1) something that persuades the reader of your case; 2) proof of what you are saying in the plan. The former is essential, the latter may be held in reserve unless it really adds weight to your case. The sort of data you may wish to include in appendices may be:

- copies of patents, copyright evidence or trademark registrations;
- copies of leases;
- detailed accounts;
- market research reports;
- CVs of key personnel;
- photographs that provide relevant support, eg of retail units if you are in a retail business or of designs if yours is a design business;
- technical descriptions;
- product brochures.

This is far from being a comprehensive list because there are so many possibilities, but it gives a flavour of the sort of evidence you may consider important.

Summary points

- List the key headings of the plan.
- Check these tell your story.
- Use appendices for the detailed evidence that supports your plan.

02
Summary

You have a few seconds to grab your readers' attention and get them interested in your proposal. They are busy, they have a dozen phone calls to make, some of which will lead on to other calls, ten emails to send, a couple of letters, two meetings and then a lunch appointment, a meeting after lunch, and their child's school concert this evening; they have to squeeze in time to write a report and work out some numbers and to cap it all there are four other business plans on their desk as well as yours. They will skim your document. However, the one thing they will read is your summary – as long as it is short, ideally only one page long.

The summary is written last although it goes at the beginning of your plan. It is the most important part of your plan.

In this one page you must sell your idea. Your audience must be sufficiently interested to read the rest of your document. In your summary you must explain yourself, your team and your background, what your business is, what is exciting about the proposal, why it will succeed, what you want them to do – to invest how much, when – and what their reward will be. Whatever the really key points are, they must be in the summary – only you can decide what they are but the minimum must be an outline of:

- the business;
- the team;
- the proposal;
- why it will succeed;
- what the rewards will be;

- any major risks and how you can minimize them;
- what you want from the reader.

You will probably refer to the market and the competition but possibly only in passing. And all this in one page! It is a tall order but it can really be done. The secret is to choose the really essential points, then to write them down and then to edit out all the bits that are unnecessary, starting with flowery adjectives and descriptions. Imagine you are standing outside your project and writing an article about it.

The one significant difference from a newspaper is that you must put the really important numbers into the summary. There may not be many vital figures but they must be there; they are the key evidence that will persuade the reader, they communicate the size of the project, the market, the investment and its rate of return to the investor. They help to fix the key points into each reader's mind. They also ensure the reader understands what the project is all about. Numbers are an essential part of communication in business.

The following example is from some 20 years ago, but it is striking how well it still illustrates these points.

Example

The promoters propose to establish a new bookstore chain to take advantage of an unexploited gap in a 1 billion retail market in the UK, having considerable growth potential which arises from demographic changes and the imminent removal of regulation. The fragmented bookshop market is consolidating into a small number of national chains and this project opens the prospect of constructing one of these. The management team have direct experience of developing and running the largest bookstore chain in the UK, with 150 outlets.

The concept is for single-floor, general bookstores in good locations in towns, where competition is currently limited and where they would be the dominant bookseller. The stores will be different from competitors in product, environment and service as well as achieving a lower cost base. Carrying around 30,000 titles together with complementary products, the stores will have the authority of a specialist, but welcoming, atmosphere to attract a wider audience than most competitors.

Single-floor units will avoid the higher staffing and building costs of multi-floor operation. A lower cost base will result from central purchasing and from the extensive use of wholesalers for supply. Administrative costs will be reduced whilst improving the quality of buying through access to a large database. By stocking a more popular general range the stores will achieve a better stock turn than competitors who also stock academic titles.

The promoters plan to raise an initial 750,000 to open three shops in the first year and will then raise a further 4 million to finance the opening of eight shops per annum, with an eventual target of 50 shops. Based on forecast sales of 300 per square foot and stocks of 80 per square foot, the stores are forecast to generate cash from their second year of operation and the business will be cash generative from the fourth year.

The attached forecasts show a business achieving rapid growth and producing attractive returns on net assets. By year five, the return on investment is 30 per cent. The peak funding requirement is 3.5 million in year four, but the promoters intend to raise a sufficient sum in the second round of financing to cover this and to allow for unforeseen problems as well as for faster growth. The promoters are investing 200,000 in Ordinary Shares themselves and seek investors to join them on the same basis. It is anticipated that investors will be able to realize their investment in three to five years through a trade sale.

As you see from this example, in less than an A4 page the summary covers:

- the market;
- the management team;
- why the proposal is different;
- the proposal;
- the return;
- the exit.

Some points are omitted: reference to risks, for instance, is not included because we decided that the several risks would take too much space – they were covered in the main document. You may decide that you do want to include a few words on risks in the summary – only do so if it provides an opportunity to show how small they are or how overwhelmed they are by the returns. Your summary is short – you want to concentrate on positive thoughts; don't let readers finish your summary with a negative thought in their minds.

Figures in the example are used to illustrate the points but their use is limited to the most important issues and rounded numbers are used. The reader will not absorb the meaning of figures precise to several decimal places. The summary is a place to fix impressions, not to go into detail.

Exercise

- Write a short list of negative thoughts an investor might have about you, your project or the market you will trade in.
- Write down your responses to those thoughts – are they convincing?
- List the really great things about your proposal that must be in the summary.

Summary points

- A one-page summary must encapsulate your story.
- It must catch your reader's attention.
- It must select the critical points and evidence.

03
The business background

What your business is about and how you got here

Nobody backs a business they don't understand. You have said something about the business in the summary but you have not gone into any detail. Then your reader comes to this section. Your audience may know nothing about your business and industry; worse, they may think they do and be utterly mistaken. You must either educate readers very quickly or put them right. The purpose of this section is to get the key facts over quickly and to paint a broad picture so that readers will then be able to understand and assimilate the detail that is in the body of the plan. You may be able to do without this section, and its substance may be repeated elsewhere, but in a few sentences it can give you a chance to get the essence of your business into the mind of the reader.

The business

I keep six honest serving-men
(They taught me all I knew);
Their names are What and Why and When
And How and Where and Who.

Rudyard Kipling

Outline what this business is all about:

- What is it, what does it do?
- Where does it do it?
- How was it established and when?
- By whom?
- Why was it set up?
- Has it been successful and if not why not?

What is the product or service?

All businesses sell something and the reader may not understand the special issues that affect your products. You must explain the key issues briefly and clearly:

- Don't explain the technicalities here, but broadly how it does what it does, and where.
- Is there anything unique about it and have you a patent or other protection on it?
- Does it have critical suppliers, distributors or customers?

The markets

Most readers will imagine they know something about all markets. You must therefore choose the important points and get them across in a really punchy way. Correct the reader's misconceptions quickly and firmly. Remember that this is a platform for saying what you intend to do and why, so focus on things that support your case:

- What is the structure of the market?
- Who do you sell to?
- Why do they buy?

- Why do they buy from you?
- How do you distribute your product or service?
- Very broadly, who are the competitors?
- How do they compete?

What do I mean by 'structure' of the market? Well, is it a monopoly, with one dominant supplier, or are there lots of suppliers? Is there a dominant group of suppliers? Similarly, are there one or many customers; one or many suppliers like you in the market? Are there segments in the market, with a recognizable top quality at one end and cheap and cheerful at the other? Is there significant branding, with one or more players in the market selling an image as well as the benefits of the product or service?

This, together with the other issues on the list, is discussed in greater detail in the next chapter.

Supply

Many, if not most businesses have important supply issues. For example, if you are a motor car distributor then clearly your plan must talk about where you buy your cars from and what influences the prices at which you buy and sell as well as the security of your supply. What are your main contract terms? If your main supplier is losing market share, then you will need to reassure your reader as to why that does not affect the viability of your proposal. If yours is a computer software business then you may still be influenced by supply constraints, in this case perhaps the supply of skilled programmers or systems analysts.

You need to answer the following questions:

- What are your main inputs? Are there a limited number of suppliers?

- Are there any constraints on your ability to get supplies when you want, at the price you want?

- Are credit terms an issue? What is your credit limit and how many days credit do you get?

Answer the key questions about potential suppliers that may occur but don't go into great detail at this stage; for example:

- Does it have key customers or suppliers?
- Does it have special requirements for key staff?
- How many outlets or factories does it have?
- How big is it? (Turnover? Profits? Staff?)

Example

Qualco is a family owned and operated laundry and dry cleaning business. It has four shops located in the suburbs of London at Shepherd's Bush, Hammersmith, Holland Park and Putney. The shops each have a ZZZ dry cleaning machine but all laundry is sent to a central facility at Shepherd's Bush. The company's drivers have a daily round to each of the shops and also deliver and pick up from customers.

Approximately 50 per cent of the business's 750,000 turnover is laundry and 80 per cent of that is contract work for some 70 hotels and restaurants in the West London area.

How did you get here?

Explain how the business got to where it is. Clearly this does not apply to a start-up proposal but would need to be replaced by more about the market and how you got involved. If the business has problems explain how they arose, what has been learnt and how they will be or have been resolved. To understand a business and to believe forecasts it is important to see how the enterprise developed. For example:

Example

Sunblast was a loss-making business acquired by John Smith in 2000 for 100,000. He cut overheads, stopped dealing in low-volume products and brought it back to small profits before recruiting new management and becoming non-executive chairman. His new MD, Charles Jones, was an accountant, a former partner with Strutt & Grovel. Profits grew to 50,000 by 2003. In 2003, Jones persuaded Smith and the rest of the Board to acquire Black Hole Ltd which was a complementary business. Unfortunately it suffered a dramatic downturn in orders owing to the insolvency of two major customers.

Jones did not report this to the Board for three months and sought to gain new customers rather than cutting overheads. Losses were 200,000 in 2004. The bank appointed a receiver and called on cross-guarantees which put Sunblast into receivership although it was still trading profitably.

In this example, which is a proposal from a management buy-in team for funding to buy a company from a receiver, more explanation would be needed. A financier would need to be persuaded that the part of the business being bought was viable and that the problems that brought the Group down really did not affect it.

For some businesses, their regulation is a key aspect of the story. Regulations may not be at the kernel of operating a shop, but for casinos, amusement machine hire, nursing homes, food distribution, road haulage, etc they are.

Dispel concerns. Your reader does not want to back a business that can be shut down at the whim of a far-off authority or as a result of a small error. Explain clearly how it all works and how your internal control ensures you do not fall foul of the authorities.

Exercise

- Write down 5 to 10 single words or very short phrases that describe your business. (For example, I wrote down the following to describe mine: heritage, travel, authenticity, expertise, range and brand.)
- List three to five factors that make your business tick.
- List three ways you could make a real impact on the market.
- List three major risks and then what you would do if they happened.

Summary points

- This is where you briefly explain what the business is all about.
- What, Why, When, How, Where, Who?
- How did you and the business get to here?

04
The market

The ideas in this chapter are not exhaustive but should get you thinking. What you are trying to do is to explain the important aspects of your markets to the readers so that it forms a background to your proposition and they will believe that you will meet your forecasts.

Only you can decide what is important and should be included.

Overview

Briefly outline what the market you compete in or propose to compete in is. Define it and explain it. The essence is, why do or will people buy your goods or services? What essential benefits does it give them?

For example, a food product provides sustenance; people have to eat. It provides a pleasurable taste. Your particular product may also be easy to prepare and therefore provide convenience. It may provide a self-image to the buyer: young, cool, sexy, etc. All these are benefits to be listed in the business plan. An industrial product, a service, anything that is sold must also have benefits that make the customer want to buy it.

Who are your customers? Describe them. It is material if you sell to an older age group that is growing, or a younger one that is shrinking. What are the problems of expanding a business in a shrinking market?

How big is the market? Unless the answer is obvious you will need to provide some indication of size so that the reader will understand what market share you anticipate. This is also a good check for you – are you forecasting an unbelievable growth in market share?

Market structure

Market structure is material to assessing the attractions of your proposal. Explain it.

For example, retail bookselling in the UK has been a fragmented industry with many independent bookshops who generally trade from small premises of less than 100 square metres, a couple of large newsagents' chains controlling 15 to 20 per cent of the market, mainly focused on a limited range of bestsellers, and chains of specialist bookshops that developed in the 1980s but were largely supplanted by supermarkets and online sales – leaving just one large chain.

On the other hand, the supermarket business has only a handful of huge competitors in most countries. Size confers economies of scale, so as a new entrant in such a market you will need to explain how you can replicate or sidestep these cost advantages.

Is the market international? Perhaps you have an engineering consultancy firm where you compete across the world in many languages and in many markets. How will you do this successfully? You may need to explore individual national markets in your plan.

Maybe your customers are international: you are a legal practice based in one country but servicing multinational clients. How will you provide them with an international service? Perhaps by merging, forming alliances or simply by being so expert in your speciality that they have no choice but to use you in one country?

Deal with problems that will arise in your reader's mind. The managing director of a big marketing agency came to see us the other day. Despite the size of his own business, he spoke of 65 per cent of his business coming from one industry-dominant customer.

One day that customer will leave him. It may take its marketing in-house, it may be taken over itself, it may go to a competitor – but one day it will go. If he was writing a business plan, he would need to address that as a priority.

Competitors

It is amazing how many plans seem to describe businesses without competitors. Even if there are some acknowledged competitors they are apparently blighted by having inferior products. At the risk of sounding pompous – just because a competitor has an inferior product, that does not mean that you will beat them in the struggle in the marketplace. Many people felt that Sony's Betamax video recording system was technically superior to the VHS system that triumphed. The European Union will license one system of high definition TV. That may be the one that is technically the best but it may also be one that is produced by a European rather than a Japanese or American company.

These competitors are people who are intent on driving you out of business. They are important. What are you going to do to get the upper hand against them? What will they do to strike at you?

Look at both existing competitors and new entrants:

- *Existing competitors*. Describe what you can about their size, strengths, weaknesses and means of operation, putting all this in the context of what you will do to defeat them.

- *New entrants*. New entrants to the market can be the dangerous ones. You feel you are tougher than the existing competitors but what about the huge company from another country or from another industry? This aspect can be particularly important in two types of industry:

  - mature industries often only provide opportunities for growth in other countries that may be less well developed or have smaller competitors;

- industries that exhibit high technological change may stimulate new competitors.

Examples that affected the UK bookselling industry in the 1990s were: foreign companies – US companies began to look at the UK market and one large corporation took over and expanded a local business – building a strong market presence very quickly; and technology – internet bookselling began to make serious inroads in this period.

Issues such as distribution, pricing, packaging and promotion, as well as how strong competitors are, are the determinants of success. It is essential to set out these issues, possibly briefly, in a business plan. A potential backer's confidence is boosted by the perception that you know your competitors and customers.

Customers

The customer is the second ingredient missing from many business plans. Who are yours? If you know that your retail car parts business serves primarily socio-economic group C1/C2 males aged between 18 and 30 then do say so. You build confidence that you know what you are doing, disarm potential questions and it allows you to say that your market is stable, growing, has high disposable income, etc. Your market may be primarily supermarket buyers and only secondarily the end-users. You need to get on to the shelves before you can worry about competing for the consumers' money. Talk about your immediate market – the buyers – but don't ignore the end-users. If they don't buy from the shelves then the supermarket buyers will not reorder. How quickly do your customers pay?

Distribution

If yours is a product or service that needs distribution then discuss how you will distribute it to the end-user. You may need to produce letters from distributors in your plan to prove that you can deliver. In many markets there are a limited number of ways to reach your customer – can you ensure successful distribution? Can you deal with powerful distributors?

You may sell directly through telephone sales, mail order or the internet. How will you promote and advertise your product or service? Can you convince the reader that this will be effective?

You may sell through agents, wholesalers or retailers. Can you convince the reader that you know how to do this effectively? Can you show that the costs of this approach are well understood and controlled?

Distribution via the internet

Virtually every business is affected by the internet, whether as a sales channel, a competitor or a reference whereby customers look at your website before buying your service. Discuss it. Selling through the internet raises a whole set of new issues, not just for your business but for the plan you write.

- How secure is your site; if your computer or your printer fails do you lose a day's business or a week's?
- Do you have a firewall, antivirus protection, good backup and encryption of customer data?
- Do you have your own website or piggyback on someone else's?
- Is your site particularly clever/well designed – and who writes/maintains it?
- Have you done search engine optimization?
- How do customers find your site?
- Are you on price comparison websites?
- Do you use social media and email marketing?
- How many 'hits' per week do you get and how does that translate into sales?

I read a story about a small business selling extra large shoes worldwide through the internet, primarily relying on one major search engine for customers. Suddenly that search engine changed its search algorithms, resulting in this company plummeting down the ranking when people searched for large shoes and its business also fell into the abyss. I wondered why such a specialist business had not built a database of past customers they could approach directly and why they had, apparently, not established any customer loyalty whether through good service or through a 'money off next purchase' scheme. If the owner had written a business plan, including, 'Ninety per cent of our business comes through xxx search engine…', wouldn't that have raised a question in his mind about his dependency and vulnerability that would have urged him to address it?

One of the big issues about internet selling is your reliance on one or two channels, while another is how fast moving such a market can be. My business sells books through the internet. At certain times of year we get good deals from our suppliers and put on special promotions when we can undercut all competitors. In the first year we did this we found the competitors matched or undercut many of our prices within a couple of weeks: by the second year we were matched within a week on all best-selling titles. We now have to check prices constantly in this market where price is critical. These issues are reflected in how you should write your business plan. It is more critical than ever that you address the vulnerabilities and the 'what ifs'. Say if prices in your market do not move much; if you use price comparison and adjusting software; if you sit in front of the computer every day and adjust prices.

Is your website intended to sell? A consultancy, for example, seldom wins new business through its website, yet most will have one. The purpose is to reinforce other, direct selling methods. Prospective customers will generally be won by referral or personal contact and then the sale is reinforced by the website which adds substance to a presentation. So talk about the aims of your website in your plan.

There are also things that are the same as any conventional business that people somehow see differently when related to the World Wide Web. I received a business plan for an internet-based business that described them as second to Amazon. Now Amazon's sales worldwide are 2,000 times larger – is that a sensible comparison? If it was a bricks and mortar business, say a family-run supermarket, would they have compared themselves to Tesco or Carrefour or Walmart – I suspect not. The World Wide Web easily provokes delusions of grandeur.

Trends

What trends are observable in your market? What changes can occur? The world is turbulent; markets are being disrupted by new technology. What are your threats and opportunities?

> 'My client produced a system to protect sunbathers from ultra violet radiation. It worked on UVA radiation which has a shorter wavelength. Then newspaper reports started stressing the importance also of longer wavelength UVB. The issue was not the technical effectiveness but producing an effective marketing response to maintain customer confidence.'
>
> (Corporate finance consultant)

You absolutely must discuss the trends in your market. These are measures of things that may be increasing or decreasing or just changing, and must include:

- market size;
- prices;
- competition;
- technology.

As well as marketing issues, such as a trend to:

- casual dining in the restaurant industry;
- casual dressing for men;
- long-haul holidays in the travel industry.

Investors like growing markets because they make it easier for you to expand your sales. However, growing markets also tend to attract more competitors which leads to falling prices. These issues need to be addressed in your plan.

Some changes can be anticipated. The reader of a business plan wants to know what might happen, however speculative. Again, by raising issues you can disarm them before they develop into a negative aura to your project. A good example is bookshops: whether at social gatherings or in business meetings, people always ask whether internet bookselling is having a significant impact or whether children read as much as they used to. There are easily identified trends towards sales through the internet and for children to read less. By including these issues in a plan, you have the opportunity to address them; perhaps observing that the internet will not take 100 per cent of the market, leaving a profitable niche for retailers; showing that the overall book market may be static but is not declining.

None of this need take an enormous effort, nor need it result in a 200-page document. A comment or a paragraph and each issue is addressed.

Competitive advantage

If you have one, make a big thing of your competitive advantage. That is the ingredient or ingredients that are fundamental to your product or service and that make you a winner.

The obvious advantage is cost. If you can produce something more cheaply than anyone else then you have a clear advantage over your competitors. You can charge the customer less or pay intermediaries more and still make bigger profit margins than your competitors.

Another competitive advantage is technological advance. The Dyson vacuum cleaner, for example, produces more suction than its competitors and has, as a result, won a UK market share of over 50 per cent.

Most competitive advantages have a limited life; patents expire, cost advantages erode as competitors find ways to match your low-cost methods. Address this in your plan also, because the reader will ask about it if it is missing. Estimate how long you will have an advantage. You may be able to claim that you will establish other competitive advantages over time as the initial one erodes. For example, you may build strong brand awareness that will maintain your market leadership after your patents have expired and competitors can copy your product.

Your business may be of a smaller scale. You may be opening the largest children's wear shop in a locality. You may argue that your advantage over other traders in the area is the extent of your range of products and that it cannot be commercially viable for any competitor to open a store of equal size once you have established yourself.

Examples of sources of competitive advantage are:

- cost;
- technology;
- brand;
- range;
- local monopoly (eg the only bookstore in a shopping centre);
- location (eg the hotel with the best view or the filling station nearest the motorway entrance);
- distribution (eg an exclusive distribution agreement with a key retail chain);
- buying (eg an exclusive purchasing arrangement with the only manufacturer).

To provide competitive advantage, your ingredient must be unique and something that cannot be copied by a competitor immediately. Ideally your differences will reinforce each other so that, taken together, it is very hard for competitors to replicate your entire system. A classic example of this is a low-cost airline which has many elements of its operation that all combine to produce a low cost base. The full-service airlines, in contrast, can't copy these elements in their entirety without compromising the rest of their business. If they try to set up their own separate low-cost division they find it is just like another competitor, competing with and taking business from the full-service division.

Your competitive advantage provides you with your Unique Selling Proposition (USP). If you have points of uniqueness then this gives you an opportunity to make higher profits, to offer a bank greater security and to offer investors a higher return.

Market segmentation

Markets often fall into different segments or niches. You may be trading in a segment that has its own characteristics. For example, you may be in the garage repair business but it is significant if you specialize in, say, Alfa Romeo cars. You plan to dominate this small niche of a large market and it is not material to you that the overall market is very competitive if, in your segment, you have few competitors, none in the locality, and can charge premium prices as a result.

If you are trading in a market segment it is very important that you bring out its particular characteristics.

Differentiation

Is your product or service different from those of competitors? Many businesses succeed despite trading in 'commodity markets'. They can only do so by selling more cheaply than competitors, whose products are indistinguishable. Or they do so by controlling distribution more effectively than competitors. But most businesses try to make their products or services different in some way, such as:

- benefits/characteristics/features;
- product quality;
- service quality;
- after sales support;
- appearance;
- image.

Explain what your differences are, because they are crucial to explaining why you will succeed. They are also crucial to explaining why your competitors won't simply copy whatever you can provide. Maybe they will but not quickly enough.

For a long time, the McDonald's corporation was happy to show its restaurants to all and sundry, even to competitors. They believed that the whole way they organized what they did was unique and that even if the surface appearance could be copied nobody would succeed in copying every aspect of their organization. This in itself was a more crucial difference than niceties of market positioning or short-term design features.

Pricing

Pricing strategy is crucial to most businesses and a book could be written on that subject alone. Indeed pricing and business strategy are intimately entwined. Whilst pricing per se may not merit a specific section in your plan it must be covered; perhaps in your description of your market, perhaps in your proposal, perhaps in your description of what makes you special. If pricing includes discounting or give-aways then the value of discounts should be shown in the financial section of the plan.

Even a bookseller who sells items with marked prices will use discounts, 'buy one get one free' offers, loyalty cards and so on which are all part of a pricing strategy. A manufacturer of computers may use price differently, perhaps pricing a basic model aggressively but charging a premium for upgrades, repairs or spare parts. They may price differently in different geographical markets or to different types of customers, such as supplying a lower-priced model to the public sector. These considerations apply equally to service industries; an accountant may provide cheap provision of tax returns but charge much more for more complex advice that arises from tax work.

Since pricing strategy is a critical competitive tool in most businesses and is crucial to their success, you must explain your strategy. Are you aiming for the top or bottom of the market, segmenting the market, differentiating your product or service from those of competitors, producing a range of differently priced products? High price and service strategies are not uncommon. The issues to be covered in your consideration of pricing will include discounting but also issues such as pack size, loyalty schemes, the provision of free 'extras' or the opposite, the removal of part of a product to be sold separately. An example of this last item would be separate charging for service or support.

Remember that the only way you can undercut competitors over the long term – unless you can afford short-term losses – is to have lower costs, otherwise the lower-cost competitor will keep undercutting you. Even with a low cost base, price cutting can be a risky strategy if the competitor has 'deeper pockets' and can cut prices in response, regardless of losing money. In the UK Virgin Trains stopped providing services on a particular route and so a regional competitor stepped in with a low-price offer, in stark contrast to the much higher prices being charged by Virgin on a slightly longer segment. Virgin Trains, a large company, immediately responded by reintroducing services and matching prices.

Barriers to entry

Banks and investors like businesses that are protected from competition in some way. Such protection usually results in protected income and higher than normal profits. A casino, for example, is protected because the law usually limits the number of casinos in a locality. In contrast, a retail shop on the high street has no protection against a competitor opening next door. I recall an instance of just such competition, where a retailer of children's clothing suffered someone opening right next door in exactly the same business.

Significant barriers to entry include:

- high cost of equipment or building brand recognition;
- patents or scarce technological know-how;
- licensing, eg a pharmacy must be licensed;
- location, eg as outlined above, being the last petrol station before the motorway both confers a benefit and is also hard for anyone else to replicate;
- access to a scarce resource, eg a salt producer located on salt deposits;
- a strong brand.

If there is something like this that protects your business from competition, you must include it in your plan.

Big changes and new technologies

Things are changing and the reader of your plan needs to know that you know that. The reader needs to know that you can cope with these challenges or that they provide you with opportunity. Much of this change is driven by new technologies but not all of it is.

Examples of market change

We all know that internet book sales are growing and that e-books are becoming more popular. How will a bookshop business cope with these challenges? But don't forget other, less technical, threats; supermarkets are increasingly stocking the best-selling books and charging low prices: their discounting is particularly heavy at the prime selling season of Christmas. How will you cope with this?

All sorts of products and services sell through the internet now, not just music and books but cameras, frying pans and clothing. Even service businesses are affected. Where a business consultant would have travelled to a client and held a seminar they now do it over the web supplemented by e-learning. Where they would have charged a day to prepare, a day of travelling time, and a day for the event the client now only pays for one day in total. Is this a challenge to the business model that reduces your income, or is it an opportunity to sell the same webinar to a dozen clients and to market it through a website, increasing your income?

You may have mentioned these changes when you wrote about 'market trends' or about 'competitive advantage'. On the one hand you should try not to repeat yourself and should try to merge the two sections of your plan; but, on the other hand, if it won't make sense to put these ideas all in one place then don't be afraid to repeat a bit.

Focus on your actions in response to change and explain:

- why a change you anticipate is not a serious threat;
- what you will do to deal with it;
- how you will take advantage of it to boost your business.

Don't fool yourself with your answers because the reader will detect wishful thinking. If there are problems you need to address them now, in your plan; that is part of what the plan is for – to clarify your ideas.

Investors have a fear that new technologies will fail or that they will be overtaken by even newer technologies. If you developed a business that used CD ROMs you will have had to address the next generation of technology. It is a perfectly acceptable approach to demonstrate that you will make sufficient profit in the short term to make the project worthwhile; another acceptable response is to show you are already planning for what happens next. The key thing is to have a plausible answer to the question and to give it before the reader asks the question.

Mixed strategies

We sell books through Amazon Marketplace and we generally try to be the lowest-priced seller of each item. However, we also compete on service and so we will aim to price higher than competitors who supply from the US, who can take two weeks to deliver, compared to our two days. We also price above competitors who have very poor customer feedback. If your business uses mixed or complex strategies then describe them.

Exercise

Write down:

- What makes your idea or existing business special in relation to its market(s)? – no more than three points
- How might competitors counter your advantages?
- What you can do to protect your advantages?
- How you can take advantage of changes in your market(s)?

Summary points

- Describe in some detail the market characteristics, its structures and trends.
- Talk about competitors and how they compete.
- What is your comparative advantage or unique selling proposition?

05
Operations

Depending upon what your business is, you may need to explain how it operates. If the reader does not understand your industry you need to explain the key factors; if they think they understand it is just as important to explain because they may be wrong and need educating. Financiers will often have superficial experience of many industries so be prepared for detailed questions; as much as anything they want to know you really understand your own business.

There are two reasons why this is particularly important:

1 Your competitive advantage may lie in how you propose to run the day-to-day business. If you don't explain this, then how can readers understand why you are different and how good you are?

2 Readers may have misconceptions of how your industry works that could affect their appraisal of it, and even if they back you, make your future relationship difficult. Therefore:

   - describe processes;
   - demonstrate control;
   - highlight differences;
   - show experience.

Let me take these out of their strict logical order in order to explain them.

Differences

Since you are trying to demonstrate that you are different and better, we need to start with the differences you wish to convey.

Let us return to the example of my bookstore business. Part of its planned competitive advantage lay in the proposal to use one or two wholesalers to source most of the stock. The benefits this conveyed were:

- less administrative burden compared with traditional bookstores buying from hundreds or even thousands of suppliers;

- computer links and dedicated systems with the wholesalers that would reduce staff time devoted to checking incoming goods into the stores;

- reduced staff time allocated to buying stock, much of which could be carried out by the wholesalers;

- improved trading terms due to direction of a large volume of business to one or two suppliers.

These are important benefits. They contribute to lower operating costs and to a more customer-centred approach arising out of staff time freed from other constraints and available for customer service. Your own business will have its own differences and benefits; list them so that you can be quite sure you bring them all out in the business plan.

You will also have to draw the contrasts with how other traders operate. You will note that the language used in the points above emphasizes this: 'less', 'reduced', 'improved'.

Processes

In order to bring out the differences you wish to emphasize, you will have to describe the operational processes involved.

In our bookstore example, the main processes are:

- buying:
  - selection of titles;
  - negotiation of margins with suppliers;
- stock control:
  - booking stock in to the stock control system;
  - returning/marking down slow-moving stock;
  - regular stock counts;
- new store development:
  - liaison with agents;
  - lease negotiation;
  - liaison with lawyers;
- store design:
  - work with designers, builders and suppliers;
- product display and promotion:
  - store display;
  - selection of product for promotional display;
  - design of promotional material;
  - planning of promotional campaigns;
  - negotiation of promotional support with suppliers;
- store management:
  - establishment of procedures and systems;
  - personnel management;
  - staff training;
  - the website;
  - channels to market;
  - managing stock;
  - social media.

Within the business plan the important elements of this mix need to be described, emphasizing the advantages versus competitors. In addition to those outlined above, for example, we identified a store design that would be brighter, more welcoming and more modern than our competitors had.

However different your own business may be from a retail chain, you can break down the processes in a similar way, to describe them and to bring out the critical elements.

Control

In describing the operation of your enterprise, devote attention to operational control. Returning to the same example, discuss issues such as:

- how stock levels would be controlled to ensure they did not build too high, swallowing working capital;
- how you will identify slow-moving or ageing stock;
- how to ensure that the stock was the right stock, ie never being out of stock of bestsellers and having an appropriate range;
- how staff overtime would be monitored and maintained within budgeted levels.

Particularly when dealing with investors, it is very important to demonstrate that you can control the levers of the business. It is all very well writing a great strategy document but the investor wants to know that you have the knowledge, the systems and the skills to make things happen and to deal with things when they go wrong. In virtually all businesses, however successful, things do go wrong and the reader of your plan will want to know that you will be aware of what is happening and can 'head off trouble'.

Experience

Experience is dealt with under the section on management. However, you will probably need to talk about your experience in the section on operations in order to provide evidence that you can run the business you are describing. The less obviously relevant experience you and your team have, the more attention you need to give to describing how you will control the business. Thus, if you are going into a completely new business area for your experience, you need to be very convincing about knowing how to run it on a day-to-day basis. If you omit something significant from your plan and then cannot answer a penetrating question in a subsequent meeting, you could be sunk.

Supply

Issues of supply may, in some businesses, demand a section of their own; in others they may come within operations. The more important and the more complex the supply issues and the more different you plan to be, the more emphasis you will need to give to supply.

In a retail, wholesale, agency or distribution business, supply is obviously very important. If there are few suppliers available to you or a complicated supply chain then you need to demonstrate security of supply. Could your business collapse if a single supplier withheld goods or increased prices? How could you deal with such a problem? What if a single supplier went bankrupt? There are lots of successful businesses of this kind, such as car dealerships. Nonetheless, you need to explain how you could cope – a car dealership, for example, may be able to switch to stocking another manufacturer's products if their first supplier goes bankrupt.

Do you have a contractual relationship that ensures your supply, for a period at least? Put a copy of the contract in an appendix if this is so and if the document is not confidential. Even if it is confidential, you will have to show it to a financier in due course.

How about prices and margins? Can suppliers dictate the price at which they sell to you or do you have some strength too in the negotiation?

For an online business, your service provider is a key supplier. If the road is dug up outside and a digger cuts your cables, what is your backup? How reliable is your hosting and what are your costs?

Systems

In some businesses, systems are crucial to success. If yours is one of those then you will need to devote considerable space in your plan to describing it. Clearly, internet businesses will require a great deal of space for systems. However, book wholesalers are also dependent on their systems – several have suffered major losses and even bankruptcy through unsuccessful upgrades of their computer systems.

For most businesses nowadays it is necessary to say, at least, what generic computer systems you plan to use or to describe the process for choosing one. In the plan written for the bookstore chain, for example, we were able to list three or four 'off the peg' specialist systems that were available for bookshops, to outline what they would do for us and to indicate the approximate cost.

Most businesses will have a website. Many will use it for e-commerce, others to establish credibility and provide information. Explain the purpose of yours, as well as key aspects of how it will work, how it will be marketed, what social media you will use to support it and so on. This not a case of putting something into the plan because it is expected; if your clientele are older and not users of social media then this may not be appropriate for you. I include it here because so many businesses are using it for promotion and for management of their brand and reputation.

Location and environment

Location is not an issue for many businesses and is scarcely worth mentioning. A firm of accountants or a computer software company, for example, is unlikely to find it difficult to find appropriate premises at an affordable price. On the other hand, for a retail business, being able to find appropriate premises at the right price in the right locations is absolutely crucial. There are many factors that could influence success in this area:

- skill at identifying good sites;
- financial strength to convince potential landlords of the strength of one's covenant;
- competition for sites;
- contacts with agents;
- attractiveness of your business to landlords.

For other businesses also, sites are crucial; leisure businesses need good locations, as do many service businesses. Tennis clubs often need to do deals with local authorities to lease land on preferential terms. This is crucial to the viability of the business but may be attractive to the local authorities in carrying out their duties to provide leisure facilities.

Considerations of obtaining planning consent from local authorities may also be important. It would obviously be unwise for a property developer to omit a discussion of planning consent from a business plan for a new marina or housing estate. But there are other businesses that also need such consents and your plan must discuss this if it is relevant.

There may be other reasons why location may be important. Some businesses need to be close to a supply of skilled labour or near to a university town. If yours is one of those then demonstrate that you will have no difficulty getting suitable premises where you need them. Some businesses, though, can work from surprisingly poor locations. We have a local florist who trades from a tiny parade of shops but thrives from their long-established reputation which makes them a destination.

Regulatory control

Your section on operations should contain details of consent that you may need to be able to trade, such as:

- planning consent;
- environmental health;
- gaming licences;
- liquor licences.

In the UK, premises that are open to the public require fire safety certificates; this is not generally a problem, but if it may be for you, then you must discuss the issues in your plan.

Are you planning to trade from a building subject to planning control? If so you must discuss the issues this raises. A hotel, restaurant or shop in such a building may have atmosphere but could also have problems getting permission for a new staircase or a new sign. Who can or might object to your plans? What impact would this have in delay or cost and how might you secure consent? Are you using professional advisers?

Exercise

- List the key steps in your operation.
- List the key features of each step.
- Write down one issue for each step that is an enabler and one that would be an obstruction.
- In a couple of sentences summarize how you will optimize the enabler and how you will resolve the obstruction.

Summary points

- Describe in detail the key elements of how your business works and what makes it different.

- Remember to explain inputs such as supply, location, skilled labour, etc.

- Deal with control; how you control operations and any external regulatory control.

06
Management

Research shows that the most important factor for investors in evaluating a proposal is the management team they back.

'A good management team can 'make it' in a poor market or a declining industry but a weak team won't survive even in a boom market.'

(Venture capitalist)

You are the team to back. You can make it happen. So tell the reader about yourselves, sell yourselves, giving the key points about your background:

- What experience do you have that is relevant to this business or project?

- What skills do you have that are relevant to this business or project?

- What weaknesses do you have as a team and how will you address them?

- What evidence of past success can you show?

Give a very brief background on each of the top management team. For each person, give their age, relevant academic or professional qualifications, experience in the industry and job they are doing or will do, highlights of past employment experience and their share stake in the company if they have one.

Put down each person's achievements and emphasize career progression. Bring out their experience, qualifications and strengths that are relevant to their current or proposed role.

Example

John Smith, BSc, FCCA, Finance Director (age 41), joined the company as finance director in 2005, having been group financial controller with Jones Amalgamated plc from 2001 until its takeover by Mega Corporation in 2005. He was responsible for all financial reporting at Jones, was closely involved in their 120 million rights issue in 2004 and was part of the bid defence team. Previous experience includes two years as finance director of a 70 million turnover mechanical contracting subsidiary of Stronson plc, during which he oversaw installation of a new computer and accounting system.

Put a more detailed CV for each person in an appendix. These should be only a page long but should give educational details and details of each employer, along with responsibilities and achievements in each job.

Some entrepreneurs are too proud to sell themselves; they give general background information but few hard facts. Maybe they are hiding something. It certainly puts the financier on guard… maybe without need. They may succeed despite this attitude but why create problems? The better the story you volunteer, the better the impression you create and the less questioning you will be subjected to.

There is a tendency among financiers towards what I call the 'Alexander the Great' syndrome. It afflicts young and old alike and it works something like this: 'We want to back people who have "done it" before.' So, if they were interviewing Alexander the Great, with a view to backing his venture, they would want to know what experience he had of conquering most of the known world. Clearly this is a ridiculous requirement and Alexander would have known how to deal with the people who set it. But on the other hand he did go into his dad's business, which removed the need for an interview. You are not in such a forceful position. The potential backers of a plan do probably reduce their risk if they restrict themselves to backing only those who have 'done it before'. On the other hand there are many instances of people starting very successful organizations, having had no identical experience; they got backing somehow. You must therefore use the business plan to persuade the reader that:

- you have equivalent – if not identical – experience;
- you have appropriate experience;
- you and your plan are so impressive that you will succeed, despite not having identical, equivalent or appropriate experience.

Never blame people for not backing you; blame yourself for not having persuaded them to back you.

Think carefully about what constitutes appropriate experience. Many people feel that experience running a small company is not appropriate to running a large one and vice versa.

Example

Julian Metcalfe and Sinclair Beecham founded a chain of sandwich bars in London called Pret A Manger. They had no experience. They came from the surveying profession. Indeed their initial outlet was not successful at first. They spent some time developing the idea, funded essentially with their own savings before being able to demonstrate a successful concept, and it was only then that they could raise significant funds for expansion and have been very successful.

Nonetheless, for every Bill Gates you hear about founding the Microsoft Corporation there may have been another dozen potential stars who could not raise finance. You can convince trading partners and investors to join you in a venture but you must be prepared to sell yourself and to shout about your achievements and abilities and make people back you as an individual and your team as a unit.

Tell the reader about your individual responsibilities if these are not obvious.

For example:

Peter Williams, Managing Director (age 52)... Has direct responsibility for sales to ANB...

Alan Warter, Sales and Marketing Director (age 37)... Works closely with Peter Williams on marketing strategy and assists him with the ANB relationship...

People are uneasy about backing one-man or one-woman companies, but nonetheless the fact is that many businesses are driven by one powerful personality – especially in the early days. Will one or two key people become overloaded? What happens if one key individual is ill for a week? Does the whole enterprise grind to a halt?

Demonstrate an effective team which can at least cope with the day-to-day issues on its own. Most venture capital companies are reluctant to back one-man or one-woman deals.

> 'I had a great start-up proposal for a publishing company, headed by someone who had 'done it before'. Unfortunately it wasn't for us... who would put all that money behind one person's judgement?'
>
> (Venture capitalist)

You can anticipate this problem by trying to set up with a partner or by having an identified team ready to join at the appropriate time.

Venture capitalists always seek references from previous business colleagues on management teams they back. Have yours ready and be sure they will say complimentary things.

'Jo gave two references from previous jobs. Both said he lacked attention to detail and one of them was not really very friendly at all. He should either have given other references or found a way to defuse the comments. His plan could have emphasized that Pete would deal with detailed day-to-day issues or he could have told us that he was not a detail man. At least the latter would have given him a chance to answer our concerns. We obviously didn't tell him why we turned down his project, we just said no and he had no chance to challenge the evidence against him.'

(Corporate finance consultant)

Whatever you do, don't hide blemishes on your CV. Most of us have failures we aren't proud of: they will almost certainly come to light and may kill the deal if it is clear that you tried to hide them. Business deals are based on trust. The people you are selling to want to trust you but if they believe they cannot then they will pull out, even at the last minute. They will figure it is better to lose 10,000 on aborted fees rather than a 500,000 investment in someone who is untrustworthy.

The essential difference

The reality is that many, if not most, businesses actually succeed with a rather different plan from the one they opened with. Things change, markets change, it turns out that those great ideas weren't quite appropriate. Never mind; as long as the management team is good they will ride the punches and adjust their plan and they will still succeed.

When I was at business school we used to study the way the Japanese motor-cycle producers conquered the world with their products. Those much-vaunted Japanese virtues were very impressive, though eventually it turned out that they weren't supermen. Indeed their original ideas didn't work very well. What was really clever was that they were open to new ideas and they adapted to meet the unexpected conditions they found.

So nothing is more important in this plan than persuading your audience that you are really good and that you will succeed come what may. Every survey of venture capitalists shows that the most important thing for these investors is... the management they back. They back people first and ideas second.

What skills are required?

The skills involved in running a business or organization differ with different businesses but generally include:

- operational (ie running the day-to-day business);
- technical;
- financial;
- marketing;
- personnel.

A plan should explain how each of these (and any others that are appropriate to your particular circumstances) is met. For example, if your proposal requires a heavy reliance on public relations and advertising skills then your plan must explain who will deal with these issues. If you intend to use an outside agency then that is fine, as long as you can detail which agency has agreed to undertake this critical task and on what terms. At the very least, if you have not got that far you should talk about how you will address the matter. The more detail and the more certainty you can give the better.

There may be weaknesses in your team. You may lack an accountant or a marketing person; you may need an IT expert. Whatever you are lacking, it can be fixed: explain how you will go about plugging the gap and when you propose to do it. Solutions to weaknesses may be recruitment, training, outsourcing or a change in organization structure. But remember that the next stage after a business plan may involve an outsider meeting key staff – they may spot the weakness you know about – so answer the question in the business plan before they ask it. If you really don't know what to do then at least highlight the need; showing that you understand the issue will encourage a partner to join you and you can solve the problem together.

Organization structure

Show the structure of the actual or proposed organization with a diagram. Clearly this is not necessary in a very small organization. There are plenty of small businesses with a managing director and no other key personnel at the outset. However, the more complex your proposed business is, the more important it is to show how the whole thing links together.

Show your organizational structure (see Figure 6.1). You are a team and an organization and you must demonstrate the ability of both. Show how the organization works and explain what is relevant. Give numbers of staff employed in particular areas to prove the level of responsibility of managers and that they are not overstretched.

Years ago, I was producing a public document designed to show how well a company I worked for was run. In doing this we realized that one of our divisional directors had no fewer than 14 people reporting directly to him. The investors for whom we were writing the plan would have been horrified since this is far more direct reports than one person can manage effectively. In the short term we excluded the diagram but recognized that we needed to address the management issue.

Figure 6.1   An example of a company organizational structure

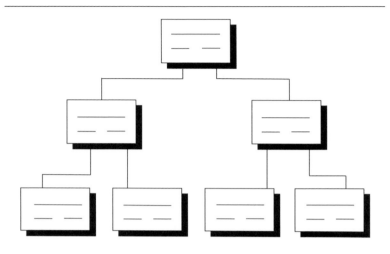

Having excellent individuals is only half the battle; you also need a team that works.

Demonstrating control

It is not always necessary to demonstrate your control of an enterprise explicitly in a business plan; it may be alluded to in the section on management or elsewhere. However, most plans will need to convince the reader in some way that you know what you are doing and can control the enterprise. This will be most important for a new business, where rapid growth or change is envisaged, or where the individuals have had any record of failure to control an enterprise in the past.

What is control? It refers to having accurate and timely financial and operational information on which to make decisions. The most basic information that is necessary to control a business is its profitability and cash flow – current and future. While this takes only a sentence to state, it is often a complex process, with many opportunities for error. The word 'timely' is also very important; in some businesses quarterly or monthly figures may be necessary, in others weekly or even daily.

Running a retail business years ago, we thought it necessary to have sales figures telephoned from each branch twice a day. Today, we get real-time sales data; I can view it online from home and my colleague has it on his phone. We have daily cash balances and account statements online from our bank. In addition, there are sales summaries which compare sales over any period and by department with a prior period or even the previous year. We have weekly branch stock figures and banking data. There are detailed management accounts within three weeks of each month end.

The term 'control' also refers to operational issues such as accurate data on quantity and types of stocks and where they are located, in order to meet demand from customers.

It may be sufficient to show, in the management section of your plan, that the team includes an accountant and someone skilled in the operations of the enterprise. If their credentials are strong enough then the reader will be satisfied that they know how to control the enterprise. However, the individuals' abilities and experience must be relevant to the particular needs of the enterprise and must match what the reader of the plan expects in the circumstances. If you cannot meet these expectations then you must persuade them to your point of view. Do you have direct experience of the industry dealt with in your plan? If not, you should show in the plan that you know what key factors in the business need to be controlled and how to do it. Often senior experience in a large company is not felt to be relevant to the much more detailed, day-to-day needs of a small business. The reader wants to know whether the finance director from a big company background is able and willing to deal with the dull drudge of the small company – where there is nobody else available to type in the invoices, answer the phone, chase debtors and delay creditors, deal with the bank, make the coffee, liaise with the computer suppliers, etc. The less relevant your past experience, the more there has to be in the plan to persuade the reader that you know what you are doing.

I was working with an old friend to do a management buy-in of a builders' merchant business he had once run but which I had no experience of. I had written a pretty good business plan, but it was based on contact from a distance; my financial background, at the time, was all with big companies and not at an operational level, yet this was a small company.

The potential venture capital financiers were concerned. They asked me lots of detailed questions about how the business would be controlled under our management, what reports we would use and how we would calculate our profits. Because of my lack of direct experience I did not answer all of the questions well and the result was that the financiers declined to finance our venture.

Subsequent experience has proven that I would have learnt what was necessary very quickly, but the fact is that I did not convince our readers at the time they needed convincing. If I had addressed 'control' in the business plan, then I might have done enough work to have pre-empted the questions that were asked later or, at least, I would have known the answers.

Computers and the internet play a crucial role in modern organizations. They provide the sort of information only previously possible by employing an army of clerical staff – and provide it faster. When computer systems are important to the success of an enterprise, and particularly when this is a new one, it will be important to explain something about them; will you buy or write the software, who will take responsibility for them. An example might be a new retail project, where computer systems are not obviously at the core of the business but play a critical role in controlling modern chains of stores. Bear in mind that people are rightly suspicious of plans involving the writing of new software. Experience shows that new systems are frequently late, over budget and don't work properly (or at all). Explain and reassure.

Control of non-financial information

The term 'control' also refers to operational issues, such as accurate data on quantity, age and types of stocks, and where they are located, in order to meet demand from customers.

As a retailer we measure footfall outside our shop and the numbers turning in and track that ratio. We look at trends in the resulting transactions as a percentage of footfall and in average transaction value, and look at units per transaction, too, and try to understand what is happening and think about what we can do to improve key measures. As a result we put fixtures by the tills to guide the queues but also to display stock to encourage impulse purchases; units sold per transaction did rise. An e-commerce business looks at equivalents, such as page impressions and perhaps even what part of a page or what product a visitor looks at. Discuss these key factors in your plan and demonstrate understanding of your market and your business.

Be aware that this can also be a trap if you do it because it is expected and do not really understand it. For example, the owner of an online fashion business tasked his marketing manager with increasing Twitter followers but without knowing whether this improved sales or whether it did so to an extent that was worth the effort. If he was writing a plan and the potential investors asked him to show the link, he might have looked foolish.

Always think about what factors are crucial to the success of your organization and then address, for the reader of your plan, how you will measure and control those factors. For example:

- If your stock goes out of fashion quickly, explain how you will know how old it is and how you can dispose of it.

- If staff or customers have a habit of pilfering in your industry, explain how you will control that.

- If stock levels are important, how will you control them? Who is able to buy in new stock and how can you control them?

Management

Stock control

The control of stock and work-in-progress is crucial in almost every business, not just in manufacturing and retail. In knowledge businesses the equivalent of stock is the amount of time invested in projects; in construction it is work-in-progress or work competed but not yet billed to the client.

You need to know how much stock you have, how much you need and how quickly it can be turned into cash. This can be the difference between life and death for the business. To do this you must have control systems that report regularly on quantities and types of stock. Do you have money tied up in slow-moving or unsaleable (often called 'dead') stock? Your plan must show that you know how to control these issues.

Example

In our retail business we had monthly accounts, available three weeks after the month-end, which showed how much stock there was. In addition there was a more informal and less accurate system of weekly reports from the shops showing how much they thought they had. Those two systems sound as if they gave good control. However, our suppliers gave us two months credit; so if our sales collapsed today and we stopped buying today our payments to suppliers would not fall for two long months. In an emergency we would pay the supplier a commission to take back stock – which is what we would explain in a business plan to demonstrate how resilient the business could be.

As a consultant, accountant or lawyer how do you control the time charged to jobs before you suddenly discover you are quite unable to charge the clients enough to recover more than a fraction of this? As a retailer how do you make sure your slow-selling stock has not got out of control?

Example

As acting finance director appointed to a machine tool business subsidiary I had to learn quickly, not only about the business but also how the accounting system worked. After a couple of weeks I was looking through some of the account headings and saw that a lot of expenses had been allocated to a particular machine that was being developed. I asked about it and one question led to another and soon the whole thing had unravelled. My predecessor had been allocating expenses to this job to avoid declaring them in the accounts and now they amounted to more than the machine could ever be sold for. The outcome of this was a large write-off.

Simple control systems would have ensured this did not happen and would have been explained in a business plan.

Control of staff

Are your staff critical to your success? If yours is a service business then you need motivated staff with a good understanding of customer needs and a strong service ethos. How do you recruit, train, motivate, appraise and retain your staff? A friend of mine is chief financial officer of a successful call centre business who spoke to me of 'stumbling to success'. However, if they had implemented professional human resource systems at the outset there might have been less stumbling. This area of control is frequently overlooked in business plans: that is a mistake.

Exercise

What skills are necessary for your business?

- Take a sheet of paper. Draw a line down the middle. In the left-hand column list the strengths and capabilities of your team. In the right-hand column list weaknesses.

- For the weaknesses, write a few words explaining how you will address them.

- Are there any areas you are unsure about; eg computer skills or ability to work under pressure? What will you do about these?

Summary points

- People back a management team:
  - show your capabilities and explain how you will deal with any weaknesses;
  - explain how you will work together.
- Demonstrate your control of the business – financial and operational.
- Be prepared to answer very detailed questions.

07
The proposal

The proposal is your selling pitch to the reader.

Explain

Clearly and concisely explain:

- what you propose to do;
- how you propose to do it;
- where you propose to do it;
- when you propose to do it;
- why you will succeed;
- what you need to enable you to carry out the plan;
- what returns you offer.

The chapter headings set out so far will set the scene for the proposal. This is where you clearly and persuasively put together your case for what you are asking the reader to do.

The proposition

The proposition is what you will do, when and how. The why generally goes without saying; you want to do it in order to build a profitable enterprise. But, where your plan is for an enterprise that has social purposes, you will need to explain the why also. The where may also be important in the context of your particular plan and should be addressed if it is material.

Give a clear statement of what you propose to do. Don't make it long and confusing. State your objectives so that the reader will understand when they have been achieved.

Objectives should be:

- *Clear*. Never define fuzzy or ambiguous objectives. The reader must know exactly what you propose to achieve. There must be no 'maybe' phrases that confuse.

- *Achievable*. There is no point setting an objective to be, say, the industry leader if the reader believes that is totally unachievable. It is better to set a less ambitious target that is plausible.

- *Measurable*. The objective must be explained so that it is possible to know when it has been achieved. For example, saying that you want to be seen as one of the industry leaders is far too vague. Seen by whom? How can you know when you have attained the target? On the other hand, objectives to establish four outlets giving you 25 per cent of the market in the London area would be very easily measurable. If you end up with five and a 35 per cent market share then it is plain to all that you have beaten your original objectives.

- *Useful*. In the example given above, a reader might ask 'So what?' What benefit does it give to be merely 'one of the market leaders'?

- *Timed*. It is important to define when the objective will have been achieved. If, for example, you propose a market share of 30 per cent but give no time period then the reader may be suspicious. If you set an unrealistic time then the reader may not believe you.

A good example of a proposal that meets these requirements follows.

Example

We intend to open a factory in Southern California in June 2006. This will assemble sugar industry equipment imported from India, which will sell to the markets in Mexico and California at a 20 per cent lower price than local competitors and build a 25 per cent market share by the year ending December 2008. Turnover in that year is projected to be US 20 million. The business will achieve break-even in 2007 and show a 20 per cent return on investment by 2009.

The investment required is US 3 million, which includes a contingency of US 1 million to cover the risk of a slower growth than anticipated. US 1 million will be provided on a four-year loan by Indiabank. We will invest US 1 million in the form of equity and we seek investors to subscribe a further US 1 million for shares to rank alongside ours.

Why will you succeed?

It may be the most important element of your proposal, a clear statement of why you and your team will succeed. What is special about you, your timing, your product, your distribution, your pricing, your alliances or the market? The reader is looking for something that is unique, that will give you the edge over everyone else.

Suppose you aren't unique. Suppose you are one of a dozen teams trying to do the same thing. Conveying your vision of a different approach or just that there is room in a growing market for all of you can still persuade your readers. At the very least, though, they will be looking for an impressive team to go with a sound business concept. You will need to persuade the reader that you are a very good team.

A team setting up a new bookshop chain in a static and already overcrowded market put forward a vision of customer centredness that was different from competitors at the time. This was allied with a team that had good experience in the trade and success in a wide variety of businesses.

However, another individual trading as a warranty issuer asked me for advice on a business plan. His business provided warranties to individuals buying second-hand cars. He couldn't show anything that made him different or that explained why he should succeed. His only thesis was – give me investment and I will expand the business. The business was making no money, had only him as a management team and was in a competitive marketplace. Merely investing money does not guarantee success. Money spent on advertising and promotion does not necessarily result in enough extra business to cover the added costs.

Ask for what you want!

Another strange thing about business plans is that people often devote enormous energy to writing them and then don't ask for what they need. This is a bit like the salesman who charms the customers and has them begging to buy and then doesn't tell them what is for sale or what it costs. Can you imagine Prince Charming forgetting to ask Sleeping Beauty to marry him? Say very clearly what you need and when, and ask for it. Remember that the written plan is only one element of your proposal. Usually, but not always, you will have the opportunity to speak or write to the recipients of the plan. Ask them again.

Some people are sure what terms they will offer to investors and can tell their readers precisely what is on offer. Be careful, because this sometimes invites a yes or no response when there may be scope for discussion and negotiation. As a rule, your forecasts should end at the trading profit line (after all expenses except for interest); leave the financiers to deal with the financial structure and what interest rate to apply.

If you know that you need 300,000 plus a three-year bank guarantee for 200,000, then say so. It is not necessary to work out the precise deal: the split between shares and debt and the precise terms. You are bound to meet someone who wants to do it differently. You may even be offering better terms than you need to. Leave it flexible for discussions.

It is not easy to go back and ask for more cash a few months after a financier has invested. Don't pare your estimates to the bone and ask for too little. On the other hand, don't ask for what is clearly more than you need; this harms your credibility. Allow a sufficient contingency for the business going better than expected as well as worse: expansion costs money too.

Repeat your need in the summary at the beginning of your business plan. Make sure readers have not turned the first page before knowing what you want and what will justify their support. For example:

> The cash forecast shows a maximum cash need of 580,000 six months after opening. Delayed payments for capital expenditure are the key to this and have been negotiated. Allowing for a 10 per cent contingency on usage, which is already conservative, the investment requirement is 750,000. This can be financed as follows:

existing directors	200,000
trade investor	100,000
brewery loan	150,000
sub total	450,000
funds required	300,000
total business requirement	750,000

> Therefore we need an investment of 300,000.

> The business is forecast to generate cash from the outset and the original investment will be repaid within three years.

What have you invested?

If there is an existing business it is important to make clear who owns what share of it and who has invested in it. You will have explained in the Background section how it has performed.

You must also set out who is investing how much in the next phase. It is enormously impressive if the managers and their friends and family will invest substantial sums in the project, so tell everyone about it. Of course, conversely, if you are asking someone else to finance the next stage of growth and it looks as though you are putting nothing in, then that is a big turn-off.

Money is not the only thing you can invest. If you introduce a patented product or you have worked for six months at a low salary and will restrain your salary for another six months, then that is an investment. Count that too. It can't go in the accounts but you can say you want to take new shares at no cost or at a lower price than other investors to reflect this investment. You can tell everyone about this investment of yours.

Do not, however, try to overvalue your contribution. You will find that other investors will be scared away if you do. Do not award yourself a large salary: that too will discourage backers.

All these things are relevant to the proposal: the reader will view them as part of the overall deal.

Second round finance

Many businesses go through another or even several rounds of financing. While that can sometimes be unplanned, it is not unusual to refer to the possibility in the first document. It may be a case of: 'If sales targets are exceeded we propose to raise further financing next year to achieve faster expansion. This fundraising would be on terms no more generous to investors than the current proposal.' The benefit of raising the future intention at the outset is to diffuse potential investor dissatisfaction if you do seek further funding. But, it is important to make a statement of this kind measured and sensible, don't get carried away with delusions of grandeur and claim a massive financing around the corner.

Closing the deal

The final element required to close the deal is to promise a reward to your readers. What is in it for them? This may not be a direct financial reward; you may be offering social benefits to a government organization or a long-term trading partnership to a distributor. However, the whole point of a business plan is to offer a reward for investment, a loan, an agreement to trade, permission to do something... whatever.

Close the deal. You have explained what the project is, why it will succeed. You have asked the readers for what you want – now finally make clear what is in it for them in return.

The exit

The return to an investor may come in several shapes: dividends on shares, interest on a loan, trading benefits to their other business interests, directors' fees, etc. But a major part of the return for someone investing in shares in a business comes from selling the shares at some time in the future. Even if the returns from dividends, etc are satisfactory on their own, the investors are likely to want the flexibility to sell all or part of their shares in the future. You will usually have to show the investor how they will be able to sell those shares. There are, broadly, three ways:

- A trade sale.
- A stock market flotation.
- A partial sale to a 'second stage' investor. For a small business this can include bringing in a working partner.

Trade sale is the most likely exit and it is usually best to demonstrate that this is a plausible route. You do not need to identify a particular buyer, unless you really are in the fortunate position of being able to offer a high degree of certainty.

A small enterprise talking grandly of stock market flotation does not go down well with most investors. Whilst it really may be a possibility, not many businesses achieve the size that makes this a viable option. It sounds all too 'pie in the sky' which has the drawback of damaging overall credibility.

Partial sales are more plausible, arising from bringing in further investors once the success of a business can be demonstrated and when further investment capital is required.

Remember, when discussing an exit, to indicate a time frame. Most investment funds will, for example, be seeking an exit in three to five years.

Exercise

Imagine that you are the investor and think through their return from their investment in you.

- A loan – how long, what interest? Do your forecasts show the business can afford this?
- Shares – what percentage would you offer? Realistically, when could they be sold? If shares were sold at, say, 5 times annual profits, what return would the investor make? Remember that while a return of, say, 50 per cent sounds a lot, if it takes 10 years that is less than 5 per cent per year.

Summary points

- Make a clear proposal, covering: what, how, where and when.
- Ask for what you want from the reader.
- Make clear what you are offering them in return.
- Avoid appearing too greedy for yourself.

08
The forecast

Strictly, the forecast is a financial matter and should come within that section; but it is so important that it demands a chapter of its own in this book. The forecast is the core of your whole plan. It tells the reader where you are going, not just this year or next but beyond. It sets out in numbers the potential for the business, your assumptions and the sensitivity of those numbers to changes in the assumptions. It explains to an investor, recruit or business partner what you are offering and enables them to judge whether the plan is credible.

The sales forecast

Perhaps not everything flows from the sales forecast but almost everything does. It is straightforward but it still often causes problems, so go methodically through the steps to prepare one.

Suppose you have four products, A, B, C and D, which you propose to sell for prices 5, 5, 10 and 15. To start with, you need to decide when you will sell what and for what price. I think the reason this causes a problem is probably because everyone knows that this is just a guess; it is impossible to be sure, and guessing makes people feel uncomfortable. Don't worry: worrying that you may be wrong can be addressed afterwards; start with your best guess. Then justify the guess with reason.

An entrepreneur came to me for help on her plan and insisted that her forecast was based on the following formula: if she spent 1,000 on marketing then in the following month her sales would be 2,000. Well, maybe, but I could not imagine an investor being convinced. If business were as simple as that then we would all be rich! The proper stages should be as follows:

Spending 1,000 will buy four half-size insertions in magazine X and three quarter-page ads in magazine Y.

This gives sales by product in the month following each insertion of: A (100), B (100), C (200), D (250).

This gives sales income of:

$$
\begin{array}{ll}
A \times 5 & = 500 \\
B \times 5 & = 500 \\
C \times 10 & = 2,000 \\
D \times 15 & = \underline{3,750} \\
& = \mathbf{6,750}
\end{array}
$$

You might assume a quarter of that income in the following month and an eighth in the month after that. In this way you show your income by month. You may spend some money on radio advertising, an email campaign or Google ads and show some returns from those too. Experience of previous advertising may support your guesses for sales. If you got business from advertising last month then it is not a bad estimate to think you will do at least as well next month – perhaps better as you get known in the market. Also, the more different advertising media you use the more you may feel they reinforce each other.

Explain why you will achieve a sales level, do not just assert that you will do so. You are trying to persuade someone. It is at this crucial stage that so many plans fail.

My client wanted to appoint sales managers but could not show any experience of what sales they would generate and how soon. I tried to persuade her to try appointing one which could provide proof to a sceptical investor. In her first forecast she insisted on showing sales generated immediately on appointment – rather unlikely. I have appointed sales managers. It takes time for them to learn your business, to make appointments and to get the right pitch. Even then a successful visit does not always result in an instant sale. For large sales the customer needs to worry about budgets and what colleagues think and may need board approval. I didn't believe it and I was on her side! Sales staff usually take a little time to become effective and even then their contacts don't all instantly buy.

Having shown monthly sales based on some evidence you can then show growth, also supported by explanation. You will get some level of repeat business, some recommendations, etc. There will also be inflation and growth in the general economy. Calculate how much these factors will contribute and in which months. Is your projected growth plausible?

Produce a grid showing your income by month. Now you have a sales forecast. From this you can work through the profit and loss account and the cash forecast. Next, you add costs to your forecasts.

Costs

You work out your costs using much the same approach as for the sales except that here you have more of a structure to work on.

The main categories of costs are usually:

- *Direct costs or costs of sales*. These are costs directly attributable to getting a product ready for sale, such as: cost of materials, manufacturing labour and a proportion of overheads directly related to these.

- *Distribution*. If despatch, commission or sales agents represent a significant cost then you may want to show this separately.

- *Staff*. Work, in detail, from the bottom up. How many staff, paid how much and don't forget payroll taxes as well as cover for sickness and holidays.

- *Property.* This includes rent and service charges and property taxes.

- *Overheads.* This covers utilities and services costs that cannot be directly related to getting a product ready for sale, such as postage, stationery, utilities, professional fees etc.

- *Depreciation.* This category can be complicated and may need the help of an accountant.

- *Finance.* This includes interest but not the repayment of loans nor bank charges that should be included in overheads.

The five-year forecast

Five-year forecasts are very useful. They are useful for scrap paper, for making paper darts and for rolling into little balls to throw into the bin on dull days.

To be fair, in some industries there is some hope of a long-term forecast being halfway accurate so far in the future. Certainly, it is always useful to show the direction you will take and what the outcome will be if everything goes according to plan.

Indeed the financier wants to see how much money might be made if everything works out. So the presence of a forecast in a business plan is not at issue. The important point is to maintain credibility and to make life easy for the reader.

Present this forecast information by having a section that shows a summary of the forecasts for one to three years: five years only if there is a good reason. Such a good reason might be a believable plan to float the company in five years, or to demonstrate how debt could be repaid in five years. It is better to show a convincing, and impressive, two- or three-year outlook than a mass of numbers that nobody believes.

Always put the summary of past trading together with the forecast, and in the same format. Don't make the reader search through the document to compare past and future.

For example:

	year	Actual		Forecast	
		1	2	3	4
Sales	product 1	100	120	130	130
	product 2	0	0	20	30
		100	120	150	160
Gross profit	product 1	20	20	25	30
	product 2	0	0	5	10
		20	20	30	40

Put detailed figures, for two years, in appendices. Nobody believes detailed expense analysis forecasts five years ahead. If someone really wants such detail, then it can be produced on request. Naturally the summary must be believable. If key ratios (such as overheads/sales) vary significantly from one year to another then explain why.

Treat the forecast as a tool for showing what will happen and why, so explain why the numbers turn out the way they do; don't force the reader to plough through detail. If there is a message, spell it out. The forecast is just the evidence for the message. For example:

The forecast demonstrates how profits will rise rapidly as turnover increases. This is because overheads will not increase as fast as turnover. The reasons for this are set out in Section...

Reviewing the plan

What do all those numbers mean?

Some people put almost no numbers in their business plan and don't outline their assumptions for those that they do include. Others put masses of numbers forward: five years of data, profit and loss accounts, balance sheets and cash flow forecasts. The mass of data is often not explained. What does it mean? Both of these approaches invite failure.

One reason for the lack of clear explanation is that the writer has not thought this through. It is actually an essential discipline to think through what your numbers are saying. You must understand your own plan. Your first meeting with a potential financier is not the time to be confronted for the first time with: 'I see from your forecast that you are forecasting a gradual decline in gross margins... it doesn't seem to be explained by the changing sales mix...'

You are also telling a story and trying to tell it clearly and simply. Don't leave the reader to spend hours on analysis and maybe coming to the wrong conclusions that may not be favourable to your case and you may not have the opportunity to explain. For example:

> *The gross profit is forecast to decline gradually from an initial 60 per cent to around 35 per cent by year four. This is due to the increase in sales through agents, at a lower margin, as explained in section three. However, we have also allowed for a 5 per cent shrinkage in margins to combat competition as the market grows.*

Try to show how sales and costs of sales are split by product. If your business makes dusters and mops, for example, and if these products have very different profitability, then show how many units of each you propose to sell and how much profit is expected to come from each.

Sensitivity

A sensitivity analysis is just a calculation of what happens if things turn out slightly differently. Using spreadsheets on a computer makes it quite easy to run these; so, when you calculate sensitivities, don't just run them one at a time. If you have been a bit too optimistic then you may have put sales too high but also costs too low and also the time it will take for you to receive a government grant too quick. In the real world more than one thing can go wrong at once. Running some of these scenarios will show how robust your plan is, but don't assume you will take no action if things go wrong. If you calculate the results of sales growing slower, for example, then you may also include a reduction in your production staff, or in your advertising budget.

If computers and spreadsheets are not your thing, you can still do some rough calculations. You do not have to be an accountant – simple arithmetic will do.

'I received a business plan for a new freight business from a businessman I respect. I had wondered, at the outset, why he was looking for bank funding when he had the money to back it himself. The forecast showed a marvellous return to the shareholders. However, after careful reading, it appeared that if there was just 15 per cent less business than forecast then the enterprise would suffer substantial loss and wipe out any bank loan.

Clearly the risk was too great for the businessman, so he wanted a bank to take the risk. Bankers are not stupid. They notice things.'

(Corporate finance adviser)

Why display the warts on the proposal yourself? Because the reader will certainly do it. If you have done the calculation yourself you have an answer ready. Your credibility will suffer if you have not calculated the risk. If you present the information yourself, you prevent the reader getting the answer wrong (to your disadvantage). You also have the opportunity to say why the eventuality is very unlikely and how you would deal with the situation if it arose.

We have short memories and, particularly when trade or prices have been stable for a while, we assume that will always be so. However sudden and dramatic changes in trading conditions or prices or technologies are not that unusual; energy prices, for example, have leapt at least three times in the past 40 years. So these key assumptions need to be tested in the plan.

Often costs that appear fixed can be cut if necessary. If trading is disastrous then staff can be laid off, although it might then take some time to staff up for recovery. Marketing costs that are essential for building a business can be cut if the sales are taking too long to respond. Growth may be sacrificed but survival may be ensured.

In the example given above, the entrepreneur had a simple solution available. If sales did not meet target within four months he would close the company and a third-party guarantee would ensure that the bank did not lose any money. He should have set this out in his plan.

When doing this review of what happens if things go wrong, pick the key factors. But there is no point in looking at what happens if the rate of growth is a little slower than planned if the real threats are that the profit margin is nowhere near the forecast or that sales per unit are lower than expected. Pick: 1) the factors that are crucial to the outcome of the plan; 2) the factors where there is most risk of something going wrong.

The reader of a business plan is unlikely to believe your forecasts and will probably assume that sales will be 10 per cent less and costs 5 per cent more. This is why you need as much evidence as possible in your plan to persuade investors or lenders that your forecasts are right. It is also why you need to show them, in advance, what would happen if things didn't work out as you predict.

Unfortunately, one business in a thousand beats its planned forecasts throughout its life and all the rest fall short. As you write your plan and work on your business, you won't believe your own business will fall short at any time. That is as it should be: unless you have confidence you can't expect that anyone else will. However, stand outside yourself for a moment and work out what you will do if things don't go quite right. That way you may be one of the enterprises that falters at the start but pulls through to success in the end, rather than being an unnecessary failure. A good way of dealing with what could go wrong is to show a Best Case, Worst Case and Expected Forecast. This allows you to influence these expectations in the reader's mind.

Key assumptions

Not all assumptions are equally important: some are crucial to the success of a business venture, while others make only a marginal impact on the final profit or cash flow. An enormous amount of time and energy can be wasted if that time is devoted to researching, say, the cost of energy for a new project when this factor only accounts for a tiny proportion of the total expenses.

This wasted time is better invested in looking at the assumptions that really matter. These are the ones that account for a large proportion of costs or revenues or where, if something goes wrong, there is a major impact on the business. This is best illustrated with an example.

John was raising money for Newco, a proposed superstore business in a sector of the retail market that had not had large out-of-town stores in the UK before. His business plan was actually very well written and he had addressed most of the key issues and many of the minor ones. He wrote that various costs were based upon detailed analysis of competitors and research carried out by himself and his colleagues – which is fair enough. However, it was clear to a reader who knew the industry that there were three crucial assumptions that rose above the detail:

- Would sales figures be achieved for a new concept, and if so, how quickly?
- Could the profit margin be achieved?
- Could new computer systems be developed as quickly, cheaply and faultlessly as predicted?

All three were clearly addressed in the document:

- For the sales assumption, John relied upon three arguments: that the market was fragmented, that assumed sales per square foot were modest and that the concept had worked in the USA.
- For the profit margin assumption, John referred to research that had been conducted to validate what could be achieved. There was reason to believe that he had been over-ambitious and it

was probably not necessary to assert that he was… 'therefore highly confident in our margin predictions'. Statements like that actually focus the reader's mind on the assumption and, far from reassuring the reader, raise a question about why it is necessary to say that it is correct.

- The assumption regarding the speed of computer development was also addressed by saying that the systems had been fully specified. This was the weakest presentation in the plan. Most of us are rightly suspicious of the ability of anyone to develop new computer systems quickly, accurately and with certainty that they will work flawlessly. It is therefore wise to give evidence to reassure the reader.

Putting aside whether John was right in his assumptions, he had clearly identified the key factors and addressed them. He did not waste time with the detail of staff recruitment, advertising campaigns, rent levels, etc. While these were not ignored, they were justified quickly and the main effort of the presentation directed to the key assumptions.

Time devoted to unnecessary detail leaves less time for crucial issues, and space devoted to less important matters lengthens your document and risks losing the reader's attention.

Check your assumptions – the reader will. Clearly set out your important assumptions and give some evidence to support them. It is important to make forecasts accessible to the reader.

It is not enough that they are correct but the important assumptions must be set out very clearly so that the reader can follow your thinking without needing a mainframe computer to recreate the process that arrived at the result.

'I recently received a nicely produced set of forecasts for a new business. The assumptions that had been used were scattered throughout the accompanying plan or were in the body of the forecast. The numbers in the cash flow were not always the same as those in the profit forecast and the two were not reconciled to each other. To cap it all, the forecast was printed out on a sheet three feet by three feet. While that did help to show three years' figures on one sheet of paper, it was not easy to use. It took me two hours to puzzle the whole thing out, so it's just as well I was on their side.'

(Corporate finance consultant)

Have a section dedicated to assumptions right by the forecast summary. For example:

1 Sales forecasts are based on 30 per cent of Oldco's sales; this is supported by existing clients who have said they will keep their business with the team, growing to 50 per cent by the end of the second year of trading, due to taking on four new clients (see marketing plan).

2 Pricing is set at a 5 per cent discount to Oldco's current level. It is felt that they will not respond by cutting prices but by trying to reinforce client loyalty.

Remember how important it is to think carefully about what assumptions we are making and to make them explicit. *Assumptions are the things we don't know we are making.*

Explain important points

For example:

1 Turnover fell in 2004 due to the disruption caused by relocating. This was more than made up in the following year as growth resumed.

2 Gross profit has improved over the years and a target of 52 per cent is usual in the industry and will be achievable now that the company is large enough to buy in bulk and get volume discounts.

Always show key ratios such as gross profit, staff costs and property costs as a percentage of sales. If these are changing in the forecast, explain why. Particularly in start-ups, business promoters may rely upon consultants' advice, but check major assumptions yourself; don't just rely on others.

'I received a business plan about a leisure business, seeking 750,000, put together by property developers with the help of consultants who seemed inexperienced in this area. I rang several people in the industry, who were happy to discuss how it worked; two were major suppliers.

I found out that the most important assumption in the plan, usage of the facility, was very optimistic. Three of the four industry people I spoke to thought the assumption unsafe. This damaged the credibility of the forecasts. Why on earth didn't the promoters make a couple of telephone calls to double-check their assumptions? They could have found out as quickly as I did.'

(Corporate finance consultant)

If the results of an assumption are a little surprising then it is even more important to put forward supporting evidence. An example of a new retail superstore business, Newco, was given above. The profit margin was particularly important to the success of the business yet the forecast margin was higher than competitors achieved, while it was claimed that pricing would be more aggressive. Published financial accounts were available to show what profit margin competitors achieved. While there were reasons why Newco might achieve higher margins, the most powerful supporting evidence would be 'terms letters' from suppliers, confirming the prices at which they would supply the new business.

Exercise

- Calculate what happens to your profit if any growth in sales is delayed by three months.
- On top of that, calculate the effect if your cost of sales is 10 per cent higher.
- Note down three things you would do if this happened and estimate their cost and their effect.

Summary points

- Focus your attention on the few critical assumptions and provide evidence to convince the reader.

- Build your forecast step by step; do not just jump to a wild guess.

- Calculate the sensitivity of the outcome if those critical assumptions are a bit worse than expected.

- Explain, clearly and simply, what your numbers mean.

- See Appendices 2 and 3 for more on forecasts.

09
Financial information

Do you need an accountant to help put this financial information together? If you do, then use one for this financial section but keep control over the overall plan. The following pages will help you to understand what your advisor is doing or will guide you if you want to do it yourself.

The amount of financial information that you need to put into the plan will vary with circumstances and depends upon:

- The size and complexity of the business that you are describing. A huge and complex business requiring a large investment will demand a great deal of detail. On the other hand, a small business might be simpler to describe and might justify less investigation.

- Whether the business is already trading. If it is, you need to include up to three years' accounts – if they are available. You must include the most recent year's accounts even if they are only available in draft.

- Who the audience for the plan is. For example, you may need to provide far more financial detail for a financier than for a planning authority.

Past trading may give a very poor indication of what is proposed, but if, for example, you have achieved sales of 100,000 each year for the past three years but are forecasting an increase to 1,000,000 next year, you must explain how such a large increase will be achieved.

A summary of trading should appear within the body of the plan and detailed figures should generally be put in an appendix at the back. The financial summary that appears within the plan must be brief and easy to follow. It must tell the story in numbers at a glance.

It is very important to include the forecast figures alongside the historic figures. Where they are separated, you make it more difficult for readers to make comparisons. In the example given above, where a sudden improvement in trading is forecast, suppose readers have to search your document to compare the future with the past; they will be irritated by the unnecessary effort and then highly suspicious that you have deliberately hidden crucial information.

There are four elements that may be covered in the financial data:

- profit and loss account;
- balance sheet;
- cash forecast;
- funds flow.

Whatever you do, don't spend ages producing a computer forecast which second guesses an investor's financial structure. You have probably got it wrong and they will have to rework it. Stop at the trading result of the enterprise and forget about interest rates, amount of equity and debt, etc: just show what cash and profit your business will need and produce.

Profit and loss account

In principle, the profit and loss (P&L) is very simple and straightforward and is the key to the success of a commercial organization. It comprises a listing and sum of its income first, then it deducts its costs to reach a net profit or loss.

In 'fairly' simple form, the profit and loss account may be set out as follows (note that all income costs exclude sales taxes):

Figure 9.1   Example of a profit and loss form

Income (excluding VAT)	A
Production/Direct costs	B
Gross profit	$C = (A - B)$
Gross margin	$(A - B)/A$ %

Direct costs

Staff costs	D
Property costs	E
Other costs	F
Depreciation	G
	$H = (D + E + F + G)$

Direct profit	$I = (C - H)$

Overheads

Staff costs	J
Property costs	K
Other costs	L
Depreciation	M
	$N = (J + K + L + M)$

Profit before financing and tax	$O = I - N$
Finance costs	P
Profit before tax	$Q = O - P$
Tax	R
Profit after tax	$S = Q - R$

What do we mean by Income or Sales? You sell goods or services but you may also receive public grants or you may dispose of assets: when these figures are added to sales income they give the total income for the business. This should be shown after deducting any discounts or the effect of any special offers (such as 'buy one get one free' in retail businesses). That is the accounting definition of 'Sales' and so your presentation must reconcile easily to that. However, if you do give customer discounts from the gross price then I strongly advise that you should show the Gross Sales (before discount) and the Discount and then the Net Sales (after discount). If you do not do this and discounts can be a significant and variable proportion of sales then your figures can be misleading to a reader. Show calculated ratios (see Financial Ratios) such as Gross Margin calculated on both the Gross and Net Sales.

The way costs are arranged in the table above is only one way of doing it – different businesses and industries will have different customs for presenting their P&L which they feel are most informative. Be sure to use the format that is best for your business. A particular example of this is the term 'gross profit', which is the trading income of the enterprise less direct costs. Different industries and different businesses within industries may have different views about what costs are directly related to sales. In manufacturing, direct costs are generally taken to include the cost of materials and the labour used to make the product. In retailing, the direct costs are generally only the cost of buying the stock but may or may not include an allowance for theft that occurs in the shops. For an ecommerce business, I would count promotional costs and website costs as overheads like rent and promotion costs for a bricks and mortar retail business.

Do note that it is unwise for a layman to try to estimate future tax bills; if you need to include this line – and I would generally advise not doing so – then get advice from an accountant or tax adviser.

Issues that may require the help of an accountant:

- *Matching periods.* It is a convention of accounting that income and costs relating to them should be matched into the same periods. So, suppose we are producing accounts for a 12-month period ending, say, on 31 December 2015. You pay a rent bill on 1 December for the three months from 1 January 2016. Although it was paid within the accounting period it is *not* included in these accounts but in the following year.

- *Depreciation.* This is the gradual diminution of the value of assets to represent their wasting worth as they get older. The most usual method is to write off the same amount each year. For example, the fitting out of a shop costs 100,000 and the business then writes this off over 10 years by charging 10,000 each year as a cost to the profit and loss account and reducing the value of the asset in the balance sheet by showing a cumulative depreciation charge that grows by 10,000 each year until, after 10 years, it is 100,000 which matches the original purchase price of the asset. The net asset value is this price less the accumulated depreciation: in this case nil. The rules relating to depreciation and the appropriate periods for writing off assets can be complex and cannot be addressed properly in this book. The key issue is how long the write-off period should be: three to four years is common for computer equipment and software, five years for office equipment, 10 to 15 years for building works. If you use the likely period the assets will last – erring on the side of a shorter life rather than a longer one – you won't go far wrong.

Cash forecast

Your business plan may show a fabulous profit projection but if you run out of cash you will never achieve it. Cash is therefore more important than profits. Businesses never collapse because they are losing money; they fail because they run out of cash to pay their bills. It is said that accountants produce profits but businesses produce cash, and it is cash that matters. The essential difference between a profit forecast and a cash forecast is the timing of income and payments. Over a very long period the total profit expected will match the cash produced. However, in the short term, you will have to allow for spending on the following: 1) equipment and computer software, which will be spread over several years in the profit and loss account but happens immediately in the real world of cash; 2) building up the business through acquiring stocks which is not charged to the profit and loss account but still costs you real money. If the timing of your cash inflows does not match your outflows then you may be unable to pay those bills and the business can fail.

Suppose you start the year with 100,000 in the bank and you have to pay suppliers and employees 10,000 each month; you expect one customer to pay you 200,000 in the eighth month. Therefore your income is 200,000 – your costs are 120,000 and you will make a profit of 80,000 ending the year with 180,000 in the bank. See table below:

Table 9.1

Month	1	2	3	4	5	6	7	8	9	10	11	12
Suppliers	−10	−10	−10	−10	−10	−10	−10	−10	−10	−10	−10	−10
Customer								200				
Opening balance	100	90	80	70	60	50	40	30	220	210	200	190
Closing balance	90	80	70	60	50	40	30	220	210	200	190	180

However, suppose the customer does not actually pay you in the eighth month: they don't pay until the twelfth month. You still make the same profit, but there is a problem... look at the table below:

Table 9.2

Month	1	2	3	4	5	6	7	8	9	10	11	12
Suppliers	−10	−10	−10	−10	−10	−10	−10	−10	−10	−10	−10	−10
Customer												200
Opening balance	100	90	80	70	60	50	40	30	220	210	200	190
Closing balance	90	80	70	60	50	40	30	20	10	0	−10	180

You run out of cash in month 11. Unless you can raise more cash, you may have to cease trading before you get paid.

Growing businesses usually require cash to fund bigger stocks, higher debtors and more staff. Profits are seldom high enough to provide all this cash, so even while you are making good profits you may need to go to the bank for more money.

At an early stage in the development of a business you may also have heavy start-up costs or initial losses. You may find that progress is slower than you expected. Again, a profitable business may run out of cash.

The cash forecast, as shown in the example above, relies upon an accurate assessment of timing as well as amounts. You can only do your best and you can be sure that your forecasts will not be accurate 12 months ahead, but your cash forecast will highlight what the key issues are for you.

Any business plan should include a cash flow forecast. It should be broken down into months – at least for the first year – and show quite a lot of detail, not just an income line and an expenses line. The reason for this is so that you don't forget anything important. Remember what Charles Dickens had Mr Micawber say:

... income twenty pounds, annual expenditure nineteen nineteen and six, result happiness. Annual income twenty pounds, annual expenditure twenty pounds ought six, result misery.

You don't have to be wrong by very much in your forecast to cause yourself a very big problem.

See Appendix 3 for more help with the cash forecast.

Sensitivity

How sensitive are your plans to things going wrong? Usually it is sales that take longer to build up than you imagined. What happens to your peak cash requirement if that happens?

You should do some 'what-if' scenarios in your plan. Prove that you can survive an economy in recession or orders taking longer to come through than expected or business not achieving your target. Businesses undershoot their targets far more often than they overshoot them: that's just life.

Break-even

Although it is just a rule of thumb, the break-even analysis gives a good sense of how sensitive the financial information is to change. It does not take account of the probability of particular things going wrong or even consider the range of things that could go wrong: these are dealt with later in the chapter on risks. The break-even analysis just states what reduction in sales (usually represented as a percentage) would bring the business to the state of zero profit.

To calculate it you need to split the costs of the business into three categories: fixed, variable and semi-variable. Fixed costs are those that do not change and cannot be changed – in the short term of a few months – if sales are lower. A typical example would be rents and property taxes. It is seldom possible to downsize the property occupied by a business very quickly in the face of lower sales because you will have a lease agreement in place. Variable costs are those, such as buying in stocks, that can be changed very quickly if sales are lower than expected and usually represent a fixed percentage of sales; so the cost of raw materials to a manufacturer may be, say, 40 per cent of the final sales figure and if sales are reduced then you cut back on purchases of those inputs by 40 per cent of the missing sales. Semi-variable costs are those that change to some extent with sales volumes but have an element that cannot be reduced; an example is electricity costs that are usually calculated on a fixed daily rate plus a rate per unit consumed.

Having analysed how these main cost elements work it is not hard to calculate the sales figure that brings you to break-even. Constructing a spreadsheet and using trial and error is often as good a way as any other and may be quicker than building a complex spreadsheet model.

It may seem to be stating the obvious but if the result is that a 5 per cent sales reduction brings a business to break-even then that is clearly a very risky proposition, whilst a 50 per cent break-even seems pretty resilient. Note, however, that even the highly risky case may still be viable if it can be shown that costs can be adjusted in the medium term and that your journey from short to medium term could be financed, maybe by you guaranteeing a bank loan for a few months.

Funding

Don't fund opening losses with bank borrowing unless you really have no option. The setting-up costs of a business should be financed with equity capital – that is, money from investors that does not bear interest and does not need to be repaid – until the business is successful, when the investors will want to receive dividends.

> 'We have come across many businesses which started with an overdraft and not enough capital. Often they run into a problem. Perhaps the bank says 'enough' before the business has turned the corner. Maybe the manager says 'no more' just as the business starts to grow and needs cash for expansion… Don't blame the banks, they have no duty to take risks, they are in business too; it is the entrepreneur who has used the wrong sort of funding.'
>
> (Accountant)

The trouble with loans is that you always need to pay the interest and the repayments even if trade is not too good or you need every penny for investment. The bank can also ask for its money back at inconvenient times. The first tranche of funding for a new business should always therefore come from investors.

Bank managers and financiers don't like nasty surprises. Try to deal with potential problems in the business plan so that you can demonstrate that they are not a surprise. It is often a good idea to talk about financial control in the business plan. Worse than a sudden downturn is one that you did not know was coming and even worse than that is not being able to show that you know your current financial position. All this can only be dealt with by having an adequate accounting system for a business of your size and type. Most businesses that fail also have a breakdown in their financial control and information systems.

A final thought on cash is that investors also want cash out of a business; maybe not at once but eventually. Therefore they will want either dividends or a sale of the business so that they can enjoy their success.

Reconciling and checking

Your cash flow forecast and your profit and loss accounts for a year should reconcile to each other. Broadly, if you take your retained profit, add back depreciation, deduct capital expenditure and adjust for changes in the working capital of the business (stocks and debtors less creditors) then you should have the figure in your cash flow. If you can't get the two to reconcile, get some help to find out why.

Remember that readers of your plan are likely to check, and errors look very bad indeed. They can undermine confidence in an instant. (See Appendix 2.)

Timing

As discussed above, one of the most important things about cash is its timing – when it will turn up to fund the enterprise, when it will be needed to pay bills and when trading activities will produce it. A business can run into severe difficulties despite the fact that cash is on its way, if it is delayed. When producing a cash flow forecast, the timing of receipts and payments should be at the front of your mind.

Sales

When will you receive payment from your customers? Are you sure they will pay that quickly? If they don't, you may be able to raise money on the security of what you are owed – this is called factoring or invoice discounting. How soon will you be paid by the finance company and what proportion of the debt will they cover?

VAT

We often forget sales taxes. Exactly when will it need to be paid? What happens if you pay late? When a business is first established you may be able to make a large claim for a refund on pre-opening expenses. However, if you miss certain deadlines, such as first registering, then the refund may be delayed for months.

Property taxes and service charges

Property taxes in the UK must be paid before you appeal against an excessive assessment. While trying to get your own money back you must cover the fact that you have to pay it – hardship is not an acceptable excuse. Also, enquire exactly when you must pay the rates – and property service charges. Are water rates and insurance included in such service charges or must you pay them separately? Can you pay monthly or quarterly?

Trade suppliers

What credit terms will trade suppliers grant you, how much credit and how long to pay? Are you sure? However well they knew you when you were working for a large company, they are likely to treat you differently if you are part of a smaller or a new business.

Professional advisers

Will professional advisers require some part of their fees paid in advance?

Taxes

It is a sad fact that many businesses hand over taxes on staff wages and salaries somewhat later than they are meant to. In the UK, delay may encourage an inspection and possibly penalties, but it does happen. Your plan should take account of when these taxes will be paid.

Balance sheet

The balance sheet is a statement of the assets and liabilities of a business. It is based on the very essence of accounting theory, double-entry bookkeeping. This tells us that any asset has to be paid for by a source of finance (liability). This may be the shareholders, banks or creditors, but if you add up all these sources of finance on one side they must exactly balance the assets on the other. That is why it is called a balance sheet.

There are several ways of presenting a balance sheet. The assets can be on top and the liabilities below, or they can be side by side. Frequently some of the assets and liabilities are mixed. An overdraft, for instance, may be shown as a negative asset. The key thing is that the two parts of the balance sheet must balance!

Figure 9.2 Example of a balance sheet

Fixed assets		
Property		100
Improvements to property		50
Plant and equipment		70
Fixtures and fittings		20
Goodwill		10
Total		250
Less depreciation		−50
Net book value		**200**
Current assets		
Stock	90	
Debtors	40	
Prepayments	10	
Cash	10	
	150	
Current liabilities		
Creditors	80	
Accruals	10	
Tax	30	
	120	
Net current assets		**30**
Net assets		**230**
Financed by:		
Shares	100	
Retained profit	50	
Shareholders' funds	150	
Loans	70	
Leasing	10	
Borrowing	80	
Net assets		**230**

An example is shown above, but someone without any financial training will probably need the help of an accountant to put together a balance sheet.

The balance sheet must balance: the assets of the business must be completely financed by shareholders' funds and by borrowing.

If yours does not balance, then work back from what happened to the money. It can only have gone into fixed assets or current assets.

Financial ratios

You should always calculate the financial ratios from the figures in a business plan. The reader of the plan will almost certainly calculate these from the figures you give and so there are two benefits for you to do it and present the information; first you make the plan easier to read and convey a good impression; second you know what the ratios are and can comment on them. This gives you a measure of control over the reader.

The key ratios are:

- gross margin;
- gearing;
- interest cover;
- debtor days;
- creditor days;
- stock turn;
- current ratio.

The reader may have an idea of what measures such as the gross margin and stock turn should be for your industry so make sure you can explain any discrepancy and also any increase or decrease in your forecasts. It is changes over the years that are most important. Why have these ratios changed or why will they change?

Lenders are particularly keen to look at gearing and interest cover. They give an indication of financial risk and of how much they have at risk compared with how much the shareholders do. A gearing figure above 50 per cent or interest cover below 200 per cent will probably give them pause for thought. Of course there will be situations where interest cover is forecast to be below 100 per cent in the short term (meaning the interest has to be covered by further borrowing). However, a case like this illustrates even more forcibly why you must take control and explain the reasons and how and when that will change.

Indicators such as Debtor and Creditor days, Stock turn and Current ratio all give a sense of the liquidity of a business.

Gross margin

This is the sales figure (less any sales taxes) less the cost of sales, divided by the net sales, shown as a percentage. You should calculate this on the sales before any customer discounts because otherwise the effect of different discounting in different periods could affect the figure.

The cost of sales is the variable cost of getting goods to a condition to be sold and its composition varies from industry to industry. In a retail environment it will be just the cost of buying in stocks that are included in the sales figure; in a manufacturing business it will be the cost of materials used plus the direct cost of labour to get it to the finished condition plus a share of production overheads associated with that labour.

The gross margin calculation focuses attention on questions such as 'Are we charging enough?', 'Are there products that we should not be selling?' and 'Are our costs rising too much?'

Debtor days

This is the value of your outstanding trade debtors divided by your net annual sales and multiplied by 365 days. It shows, on average, how quickly your customers are paying you. Clearly there is a measure of seasonality in this and you could try to correct for this, perhaps by taking sales over a shorter period and multiplying by that number of days, not 365. I think that, in most circumstances, that is probably over-sophistication: this ratio just gives a quick idea and if it is misleading just explain why and move on.

Ideally your debtors will pay you more quickly than you pay your creditors. If not, why not?

Creditor days

This is the value of your outstanding trade creditors divided by your annual cost of sales and multiplied by 365 days. Why should anyone care how long you are taking to pay your bills? Because if your plan shows you are taking longer to pay it could be because you are running short of cash and using the creditors to balance your figures. As stated above – ratios pose questions rather than giving easy answers.

Why is it restricted to trade creditors? Because you don't usually have much discretion over when you pay utility bills and the like, so including these distorts the picture. Also such costs are not included in the cost of sales.

Stock turn

This is the value of stocks, at cost, divided by the annual cost of sales and multiplied by 365 days. It excludes the profit margin because profit is not included in the value of stocks in the accounts. It is a measure of how much cash you have tied up and can signal ageing stocks that are becoming hard to sell.

Current ratio

This is the ratio of current assets to current liabilities shown in the accounts. It is usually expressed as a decimal but can be shown as a percentage. If the figure is less than 1 or 100 per cent it indicates that you are using your suppliers' money to run your business. Really only supermarkets or other large fast-turnover businesses achieve this and they expect the stock turn to be high too.

Gearing

This is the net debt (that is debt less cash in hand) the business has, divided by the sum of that debt plus shareholders' funds. It tracks how much debt (usually including bank, leasing and any debtor factoring) the business has and can indicate both shortage of cash if it is on a rising trend but also the financial risk in a business. The higher the gearing the greater the risk.

Interest cover

This is the pre-interest profit divided by the interest shown as payable over the same period in the accounts, expressed as a percentage.

Other measures

Labour as a percentage of sales; overheads as a percentage of sales and, for some businesses, property occupation costs as a percentage of sales can all give a useful feel for trends. Clearly you want to show falling labour costs, overheads and property costs together with rising margins but don't force the figures to try to paint a false picture.

As noted above, all these measures are industry specific and can even be company specific. A software house, for example, may have sky-high margins because so much of their cost base is devoted to product development; so it might be wise to include a proportion of those development costs in the cost of sales and in stocks, giving a lower margin.

The phrase Key Performance Indicators (abbreviated to KPIs) is used extensively – often by people who have bizarre ideas about which financial ratios matter and why. If they knew more about practical accounting they would have less blind faith – still, you know your business and, I hope, you know which numbers you should be tracking. Stand your ground and explain that the indicators you follow are the relevant ones for your business.

Trends

In discussing risks we have referred to trends in the figures. Just as it is important to consider what can go wrong it is important to think about the direction of change of key indicators and to explain them. If your commentary talks about economies of scale then the reader will be looking to see rising margins and, if the figures don't show that, you must explain why. So check that the ratios make sense and reconcile with the commentary and the trends. Don't show trends that don't make sense. For example, many business plans for existing businesses show steady sales levels or profit levels in the past but suddenly transformed in the forecast to show a dramatic increased trend. Either moderate your forecast or make sure you convincingly explain the sudden shift in gear.

If you are showing a sales forecast that looks like this, your readers will be sceptical – persuade them.

Figure 9.3   The 'dogleg' graph

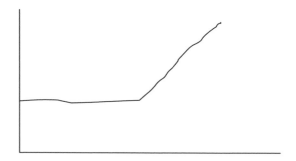

Some important terms

Goodwill

Goodwill arises where a business buys another for, say, 100 but its balance sheet shows net assets of 80. The difference of 20 is termed goodwill. It is assumed that you haven't paid the extra 20 for nothing. Accounts value the business you have bought only at what its balance sheet says, although you have paid extra for the future profit potential.

Accounting standards require goodwill to be written off a bit each year. If this affects you then you may need advice from an accountant.

Prepayments

On the principle of matching income and expenses within the same period, you will generally show a payment in advance as a debtor. So, if your year-end is June and you have received a bill for rent in May that actually relates to July, August and September, it will not figure in your profit and loss account but will be shown in your balance sheet as a pre-payment – even if you haven't actually paid it yet. If it is received and it is dated May then you must enter it into your accounts as a creditor (which is a liability), but then it is also shown as a pre-payment (which is an asset) so that the two halves of your balance sheet balance. If you do pay it in advance then it no longer appears as a creditor but reduces the cash in your business, though it still appears as a pre-payment.

Accruals

You will sometimes allow in your balance sheet for a bill that you know is on the way but which has not yet arrived. This reflects the accounting principles of matching but also of prudence. So, if you have not received an electricity bill for a year you will assume that the electricity company has made a mistake. However, they may catch up with you one day, so you charge the anticipated bill as an expense but show the balancing entry as an accrual (creditor).

Pro-forma balance sheet

A pro-forma is a highly simplified set of accounts shown to reflect a theoretical position. The words 'pro-forma' tell the reader that the figures are an illustration and are not a forecast. So a new business will have a pro-forma opening balance sheet. It will probably have no debtors or creditors, because it gives a snapshot before it starts trading. It will just have assets and cash balanced by shareholders' funds and borrowing.

Similarly, a pro-forma balance sheet is prepared for the acquisition of another company or the addition of a new business or the results of a rights issue, showing a simple adding together of the overall assets and liabilities to give an idea of what the merged balance sheet would look like. It is also possible to produce a pro-forma profit and loss account to show what the theoretical trading results would have been for a trading period incorporating two businesses that are to be merged (or incorporating a new business to be started).

Exercise

- List three or four Key Performance Indicators for your business.
- Write a couple of sentences for each to explain why they matter.
- Calculate these KPIs using your forecasts (and past figures if the business is already trading).

Summary points

- Every business plan needs financial information to back up the words.

- Do you need help from an accountant to put together the financial information?

- The words and numbers must tell the same story.

10
Risks

Risk is often dealt with in the section in your business plan dealing with forecasting. The logical place to insert it is after detailing the assumptions in the proposal. Why talk about risk? Because by raising the issue you own the conversation: 1) You show that you appreciate there are risks to your business proposal, as with anyone else's. If you pretend yours is a risk-free proposal then neither investors nor business partners will take you seriously. 2) You have the opportunity to deal with the concerns that will come into your reader's mind. You pre-empt questions and, in doing so, strengthen your case.

There are several ways of dealing with risk. For example, you can:

- demonstrate that the probability of something happening is small;
- show that the impact of the event would not damage the business seriously;
- explain how you would respond to adverse circumstances.

In the example of the bookstore chain, some anticipated risks were:

- economic downturn leading to sales, say, 15 per cent below forecast;
- the main supplier proving unwilling to continue to supply;
- greater competition than expected leading to sales, say, 15 per cent below forecast and the gross margin 2 per cent lower than forecast;

- costs turning out to be 20 per cent higher than forecast;
- borrowing costs rising 5 per cent.

As you see, there are generally only four types of risk:

1 that sales are low;

2 that margins are low;

3 that costs are high;

4 that a major operational problem occurs.

Of these, business plans usually get the first two wrong rather than the last two. It is unusual, though not unknown, for costs to be very significantly higher than expected. As long as you have done a reasonable amount of homework you are unlikely to get the total level of costs dramatically wrong. This is because, to have a significant impact, you would have to get one or two elements of cost hugely wrong. For example, if the accounts of a retail business look like this, as a percentage of sales:

Gross profit	45%
Less:	
Staff costs	15%
Property costs	15%
Other costs	5%
Profit	10%

to get total costs wrong by 10 per cent of sales, which leaves you at break-even, you would need to have the cost of sales out by 18 per cent but staff costs out by 66.7 per cent to achieve the same effect.

You should focus on discussing the risk of getting sales or margin wrong. What could happen and what would the impact be? Don't list dozens of things that could go wrong: depending on your business there are unlikely to be more than six or eight significant risks – deal with these. Always explain what you would do to avoid the event occurring and to deal with it if it occurred. Low margins, for example, might be addressed by targeted promotional activity, reconsidering the sales mix or raising prices (albeit at the cost of losing sales). Never say in your plan that you will raise prices without recognizing that you will lose sales, because this will undermine your credibility. If you can raise prices without losing sales then why don't you do that anyway?

The final type of risk to address in this chapter is a major operational problem such as theft or fire, failing to get planning consent, losing your main supplier or a fundamental breakdown in your production process. As far as possible you must address these issues by showing that you have insurance permits or contracts in place, that you have alternative sources of supply or that you can deal with a breakdown in production, albeit at some cost.

Business is never without risk. Your investor or prospective partner will understand that the rate of return you are promising reflects a reward for taking risk. So after you have explained, as far as you can, how low the risk is and how you will deal with it, don't worry about there being some risk that you must admit to but that you can do nothing about.

What did we get wrong?

Learn from the mistakes of others. We got the threat from online bookselling about right, in the short term, but we did underestimate the market share they would eventually achieve. However, we missed the impact of supermarkets hugely discounting bestsellers at the peak sales period of Christmas and we lost out to timing; competitors had entered the market just before us and were always beating us to the best retail sites, forcing us to take the risk of secondary sites.

Long term versus short term

In order to get to the long term you need to survive the short term. Do not waste too much energy worrying about the 10-year horizon because you have plenty of time to adapt and diversify if you make a big success of the first three years of your plan! So mention the far distant threats (and opportunities), but focus on those that will get you long before.

Focus on the big stuff

Apply the 'DIM' principle – Does it Matter? I put forward a capital expenditure plan to replace our computer servers before the peak trading season because I was worried about the resilience of our systems. The probability of failure was small but a recent small-scale failure had shown that the consequences could be big. So this was a strategic decision, dealing with how we should operate. I got back an unexpected response to my proposal: whilst there was immediate agreement in principle, the board delayed a decision in order to deal with the financing of the project, and by delaying prevented a solution being in place when it really mattered. The reason was that they had focused not on the big issue but on a side issue – financing was not a problem and our cash flow would cover the expenditure. The lesson is to express your plan to focus the reader on the big decisions they must take and to de-emphasize small issues. Think about how your reader will react and guide them in the right direction.

Don't forget the everyday stuff

Today almost every business has a systems risk. Don't focus on these and ignore all the other business areas. But, likewise, don't forget systems – your computer servers could catch fire, your software provider could become bankrupt, your data could be hacked or be hit by a virus – leading to loss of client data, deletion of files or complete loss of access to files. You could lose electric power or internet access for weeks. Don't just worry about data also think about how quickly normal operation could be restored.

Virtually all businesses have an online presence, all use computer systems. Is cybersecurity a risk? Are you backed up? Is your software up to date? Are you insured? If your lease line went down do you have a backup system? Are you critically dependent on a particular software house: what would you do if they went out of business? Are you compliant with data security legislation?

But think about the mundane too: a neighbouring business retails high quality chocolates. They suffer a burst water pipe that prevents them from trading for eight weeks over Easter. Insurance covers immediate losses but what about customers going elsewhere and never returning? Do you have insurance to cover 'consequential loss'?

What about people? Are there key people whose loss would be catastrophic?

I would like to share an example from a plan presented to a company board. The final sentence read: 'While the risks are significant, no alternative plan has been tabled for consideration.' Who on earth thought that writing that was a good idea? My response, on reflection, might have been more sensitively drafted, but the sentiments I expressed were absolutely on the mark and I commend them to the reader's attention. I wrote: 'The suggestion appears to be to close our eyes, hold hands and jump into the abyss 'cause nobody has any better ideas? I respectfully bring to everyone's attention our legal responsibilities as directors, as well as our moral responsibilities to employees and stakeholders, to use our best efforts to make reasonable enquiries before taking decisions.'

Exercise

- List every risk to your proposal and group them into the four categories of sales, margins, costs and operational.
- List these risks in a table and evaluate for each one the probability of occurrence (low, medium and high); the consequences of occurrence (minor to devastating); what you could do if each occurred; and whether it's a short-term or long-term risk.
- Below your table, write three sentences to describe what would happen if more than one risk event occurred simultaneously.

Summary points

- Every business has risks.
- Explain what your main ones are and how likely they are to go wrong.
- Above all, explain (briefly) how you will deal with things going wrong.

11
Legal issues and confidentiality

Confidentiality

There are important legal issues that arise from sending someone a business plan or a sale memorandum if they are neither professional investors nor a financial institution nor professional advisers. There are also issues that arise from sending any plan to anyone if it may result, in due course, in a deal of some sort being done. For example, UK law now states that your document may be a prospectus, which would require an accountant's report on everything in it. This is all very well if yours is a big business but seems a bit excessive if it is not. The risk becomes almost a certainty if you send the document to 50 or more people. In addition there is a risk that someone either invests in or buys your business, having read your plan, things do not go well and they sue you for misrepresentation based on something that was in the plan.

In order to avoid these risks you may be well advised to consult a lawyer who will draft a suitable letter for the recipient to sign and a preamble for the plan itself. The letter will get the recipient to acknowledge that they are a sophisticated investor, or a high net worth individual, or that they are getting professional advice. The preamble to your plan will try to insist:

- that the document is an information memorandum and not a prospectus (the latter word will not be used) and certainly not an offer for sale;

- that the document shall not form a part of any contract;

- that the directors and shareholders of the business are not giving any warranties or guarantees that the information contained in the document is accurate;

- that the recipient will not rely upon the document but will make their own enquiries about the business.

A little while ago I received a sale memorandum about an internet business which contained all these clauses but I was amused to see that the people trying to sell the business were trying to get both an indicative price as a result of the document and also to restrict the ability of a potential purchaser to make full enquiries (often called due diligence) about the business. I strongly suspect that such an approach would compromise the claim that the original document was not an 'offer for sale' – I don't see how you can have it both ways. They were clearly copying someone else's document they had got hold of. This also highlights another issue: whilst you may want to copy someone else's preamble or covering letter, do be aware that the law may have changed since it was written or that the circumstances may be different than envisaged by whoever wrote theirs; they may even have copied their covering letter from someone else in turn. You are safer getting legal advice: if you don't, at least be aware that you are taking a risk.

Whether a business plan is sent to a prospective business partner or to a bank or to staff, there is often an important issue about the confidentiality of the information in it. Some people and businesses steal the ideas of others and, if you don't have the time or money to pursue a court case, you may be powerless to do anything about it. There are several ways to reduce your risk:

- Get recipients to sign a confidentiality agreement.

- Insert a paragraph at the front of the plan that binds the reader to secrecy.

- Try to omit sensitive information.

The last option is often not realistic; a bank, for example, will be unimpressed by a plan that omits the cash forecast if you are seeking a loan. An investor will wish to see a key supply agreement. However, it may be possible to hold back some information while you establish trust with a prospective business partner.

The confidentiality agreement can vary between a typical half-page letter to the five- or six-page document that some merchant banks issue when they are selling a business. It all depends upon the circumstances. An example of a fairly simple letter is given in Appendix 1. However, this is only an example and if you are concerned about confidentiality you should consult a lawyer.

The agreement will usually cover:

- Defining the information that is being given and stating that it is valuable and that its communication to unauthorized people will damage the business. (*It will usually emphasize that only information that is not 'in the public domain' is covered.*)

- Binding the recipient of the information:

  - to keep it confidential;

  - not to make use of the information in their business (this is particularly important when you may be in discussion with a potential competitor);

  - only to pass the information to their staff and advisers and to bind them in the same way as they have agreed with you.

Some confidentiality agreements will state that the recipient will not approach customers, suppliers or staff of the business giving the information. They may undertake not to enter the same business. All such undertakings will usually have a time limit on them. If you set what the courts might feel to be an unreasonable constraint they may not enforce it. Agreements frequently require the recipient not to make or to return any copies of the plan at the end of discussions. I have never understood how this can be enforced, nor what can be done if the recipient is found not to have complied.

Where the confidentiality undertaking is part of the plan itself it will come at the front and state that by accepting the document the recipient agrees to be bound by the undertaking.

Before leaving the subject, note that legal action to enforce confidentiality undertakings is rare and, because of the cost, a bigger proportionate burden to the smaller business. Disputes seldom reach court unless they are for sums in excess of 50,000, in the UK, and if they do there is a risk that the other side will apply to the court for security for their costs. This allows big businesses to bully smaller ones because, if you feel there is a risk of losing (... and there is always risk in going to court) both parties' legal expenses could add up to a very frightening sum. Even finding the security to post with the court may be a significant burden for some.

Exercise

Are any of your business ideas truly original?

- List your original ideas.
- Break each item into its elements and focus on the particular elements that are most valuable.
- For each one list possible ways to protect them from being copied.
- Are there any details you can delay sharing?
- Do you trust the people reading your plan?
- Have you researched the individuals?

Summary points

- Don't give your valuable information to people you don't trust.
- You can try to protect your ideas with a confidentiality agreement but recognize that these are hard to enforce.
- Don't give information that someone can sue you about if you prove to be wrong.

12
Selling your business

The business plan is often used to sell a business. You may employ an accountant to do this for you and they will generally write the business plan or sale memorandum, which is the same thing in this context. However, even if someone else is doing this for you it is still useful to have an idea how it should be done so that you can influence and check their work.

The document is essentially similar to the business plans described in this book. In place of the summary that a business plan has at the start it will start with an 'Investment Proposal' which will briefly summarize what the buyer is being asked to do, what the business is and what its main sales features are. It will then swing into an 'Introduction' that describes the business. Sections on the market, management and financial record follow.

If the process is so similar what is different? The main differences are tone and what is omitted such as detailed strategy and 'people plans'. I was recently sent a sale memorandum for an internet business that provides a number of examples of what not to do as well as a few interesting points.

Explain why you are selling

If you don't tell the buyer why you are selling, and unless what you say is convincing, expect them to draw their own conclusions, which may not be to your liking. They may decide that the business is deteriorating and that you are desperate to offload it.

Emphasize the great opportunities for the business

But note the point above. If the opportunity is so great, why are you selling? Therefore your line must be something such as: that you believe this is a good time to make a profit and head for a retirement villa; that you believe a buyer can make a lot more money than you; that you don't have the resources to develop the business as it deserves.

Don't waste time illustrating that sudden upturn in business expected imminently

While it is important to emphasize the great opportunity open to the buyer, it is really not a good idea to go 'over the top'. The memorandum I received showed sales and profits going as shown in Figure 12.1. Isn't it odd how sales and profit in the future always seem to take a sudden upward leap? There is one exception to my admonition to avoid this sort of unbelievable forecasting: when there really is some reason to believe that business is going to rise rapidly and a persuasive case can be put forward to support this and where there is also a plausible explanation for your desire to sell just before this happens rather than afterwards; then and only then should you feel it helps your case to include a forecast like this in your sale memorandum.

Figure 12.1 Sales and profit by year

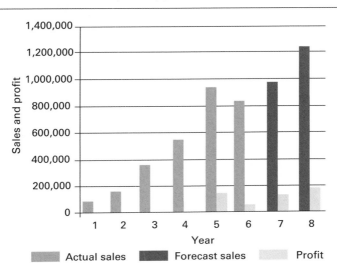

I strongly believe that a buyer is put off by such nonsense and that they lower their possible price to adjust for the extra risk they perceive from both the seller's desperation to make a good case and from distrust of what they are being told. In this case it was also clear that the numbers quoted excluded some pertinent costs so that relatively modest profits were, in reality, even more modest.

Do you include a forecast?

If you have a forecast or a budget then I do think it is worth including it in the plan but do explain the assumptions and exclude the more ridiculous ones: a forecast that the reader does not believe is not worth including. The internet company quoted above admitted the loss of a major customer but assumed in their forecast that they would win extra business to replace them in the following year. Oddly the sales and profit were budgeted to fall 29,000 in the current year but forecast to bounce back by 30,000 in the following year. Well yes, maybe. They failed to give the detailed explanation that would lift this assertion from the status of 'nonsense...' to 'yes, that sounds reasonable...' Of course you should talk up your business but you must give plausible and detailed explanations if you do that.

Who is the buyer?

You probably don't have the luxury of the time required to write different documents for different buyers so think about their needs at the outset and try to write something that will cover all of them. If there are any significant differences that you can't really address in one document what about dealing with this in the covering letter you send with the sale memorandum? The sellers of the internet company described here did think about potential buyers and listed some possible categories of buyer in their document but then, having identified 'people new to internet businesses', they did not give a sufficiently detailed explanation for them. For example, such people would, by definition, not have programming skills yet the sellers failed to explain where the programming skills resided in their company. I think they sub-contracted such things but am still not sure. Identify your buyer and then address them!

Holding back information

If you are selling a business, the reader of your document is very likely to be a current or future competitor and some of the apparently interested parties may well just be fishing for information. How do you avoid giving them sensitive information? I have described confidentiality agreements elsewhere in this book and clearly you will try to keep back information that is particularly useful to a competitor until late in the sale process. Your initial sale memorandum will not include everything the buyer may need and you may ask for an indication of price before giving further information to one or two interested parties. Remember that you will have to tell them eventually, and that you can carry caution too far.

The sale memorandum is a tool to sell the business and to maximize the price you get. Do not hide information that really does not matter that much to you: it is easy to be over-secretive. Our internet company did not reveal the split of sales revenues between different types of business. I really don't understand why this should have been sensitive and I really wanted to know in order to assess the opportunity. In the end we were not one of the bidders.

Due diligence

The business plan that is written with a view to selling a business is likely to be the subject of due diligence. That means that all the data and all the assertions that are included in it are likely to be checked by a prospective purchaser, which means you must take even more care to get it right first time. In preparation for that it is a good idea, when you have finished it, to analyse the plan on your computer screen, arranging extracts from it in a table with each assertion or table or set of figures on the left hand side and supporting evidence on the right. If there is anything that is opinion then make sure it is stated that it is opinion. If there is anything that you are saying is a fact but that you cannot produce evidence to support then consider rephrasing it or omitting it. Although your plan will probably be delivered with a caveat that a purchaser must check everything for themselves they may still try to get you to provide a warranty that everything in the plan is accurate. You probably cannot avoid giving a limited warranty that past annual accounts were correct, or that relevant taxes have been paid, or that the business has not engaged in illegal behaviour.

Do you own what you are selling?

People think about equipment or premises when they list the valuable property of their business, but what about intellectual property and goodwill?

You have your trading names, possibly unique processes, images, written material. Do you own them? Do you have patents, copyright or trademark protection? If you do have protection, is it worldwide or just local?

Do you use someone else's intellectual property in your business, and, if you do, can the business automatically continue to use it if control of the business passes to someone else?

Goodwill sticks to trading names and expresses the value arising from customers identifying with and being influenced by that name, image and reputation. All easily lost to scandal. Does your business have any hidden issues lurking? Any business transfer gives rise to undertakings in the legal contracts.

Exercise

Write another list:

- Why do you want to sell?
- Do you want to retain an involvement?
- Why will a buyer want the business? What sort of buyer?
- How can the buyer make more money from the business than you can?

Summary points

- Think about your reader and include what they will want to know while holding back what you don't want them to know until they have made a firm commitment.
- Don't oversell; if it is so fantastic, why are you selling?
- You may have to substantiate any claim you make – can you do that?

13
Improve business performance

A business plan is an essential management tool to assist in running all sorts of organizations, ranging from businesses, through charities to public sector bodies. It is not just for organizations setting up but for those that are established as well. A written plan is just as important for an entrepreneur as for a division of a multinational company or a hospital trust. This section looks at how they are useful, how they are different from (and how they are the same as) plans drawn up for investors, and how to construct them.

Planning is not budgeting

How to use plans to help run your organization

There are six important ways in which a business plan helps to run an organization:

- strategic direction;
- performance management;
- performance measurement;
- coordination and control;
- communication;
- empowerment.

Strategic direction

Don't use the business plan in an attempt to find a new strategic direction. The discipline that is the essence of planning inevitably shuts down free-ranging thought – which is of the essence of strategic thinking – and is therefore unsuitable for delving into completely new directions.

It is a common misconception that a formal business planning process and the discussion and analysis that this usually involves provide managers and business planners with their strategy. In practice, this is rarely the case, for strategy is not the consequence of planning but the opposite: its starting point. 'Planning helps to translate intended strategies into realized ones, by taking the first step that can lead to effective implementation' (Henry Mintzberg, *The Rise and Fall of Strategic Planning*, 1993).

> … its planning did not give this company an intended strategy. It already had one, in the head of its entrepreneur, as his vision of its future. That is what encouraged it to go to financial markets in the first place. Rather, planning was the articulation, justification and elaboration of the intended strategy the company already had.
>
> (Henry Mintzberg, *The Rise and Fall of Strategic Planning*, 1993)

However, through a thorough review of objectives, resources, markets, strengths and weaknesses, options, etc some individuals and teams *will* formulate new directions – they may also discard previous intentions, which are shown to be unworkable. These strategic ideas can then be worked on outside the formal planning process.

Performance management

A business plan is the starting point of a performance management programme. It ensures that everyone is working in the same direction and it can be used to establish individual goals and work plans for the period it covers. It can be used to:

- set objectives – both for departments and individual performance objectives;

- identify objectives or strategies that may be incompatible; for example, there may not be enough money available to carry out both customer service training and team building;

- set priorities;

- identify training and development needs that will ensure your workforce has the knowledge, skills and abilities to achieve success;

- focus training and development on the achievement of business goals.

Performance measurement

It is vitally important that the business plan contains clear, measurable goals. A recognized technique for drawing up goals is to use the SMART criteria:

- Specific.
- Measurable.
- Agreed.
- Realistic.
- Timed.

The chief executive of one organization became a virtual laughing stock amongst his team when he announced his grandiose intention to become the market leader. They knew that the statement was just hot air – they were miles away from market leadership. Under the SMART criteria, his vision may have become something like:

To increase our market share from 20 per cent to 30 per cent over the next three years.

A crucial step in using the SMART criteria is knowing how to achieve the goals – without this component the goals cannot be agreed and you don't know if they are realistic. An example of 'how' might be:

> To increase levels of customer satisfaction by reducing delivery times to an average of seven days within 12 months, to be achieved through the construction of a distribution depot, the introduction of new scheduling software and retraining of the scheduling department.

Coordination and control

The business plan can be used to measure business or departmental performance against the objectives and milestones that have been established. The comparison can be used to refine and redefine your objectives and timescales.

The objectives established for an overall business lead on to setting objectives for the departments and activities within the business that will support the achievement of that overall plan.

Example

The senior managers of the UK subsidiary of a large US-based multinational agreed a five-year plan. Its central objective was to achieve 20 per cent per annum growth across the whole business. Since one of the geographical areas covered mature markets with potential growth of no more than 10 per cent, this focused attention on what actions could be taken in other divisions to meet the overall objective.

Communication

In many ways communication is the most important role for an internal business plan:

- Amongst the top team it provides a focus for them to get together to discuss and make decisions, to share ideas, to clarify each other's roles and maybe to bring out and deal with any underlying conflicts.

- A larger organization should get the next level down and possibly even the level below that to contribute to the development of the plan. This creates ownership and makes for a better quality plan, as well as providing communication and team-building opportunities.

- Note that one of the most common failures of planning occurs when senior managers plan in isolation, little realizing that they no longer have the understanding of the customer and customer dynamics that they once had. You must have the input and involvement of people who are in direct contact with the customers and you will need it at an early stage.

- There are many advantages to be gained by disseminating the final plan throughout the organization. Managers and staff alike can see the business, the market and the whole context of their organization set out and explained. They understand the direction the business is taking:

  - This helps to build pride in their business and their contribution to its success.

  - Through understanding where the business is going and their place in that strategy, people make better day-to-day decisions that take the business towards its goals.

  - It promotes openness and trust and helps morale.

  - It often results in useful ideas being generated at all levels in the organization.

  In total, all these effects can end up by making a dramatic and positive difference to the effectiveness and profitability of organizations.

Remember that all effective communication leads to changed behaviour. There is no point to it if there is no effect. A business plan with clear, measurable objectives provides the agenda for communication in an organization. You communicate the goals first and then keep communicating progress against them. As you progress, you can celebrate success and communicate where and how to focus effort on areas that need improvement.

Do not be concerned about writing down and circulating strategies because they might be leaked to competitors by disloyal staff: this is seldom a realistic fear. You can omit sensitive information but how can you manage your staff without telling them what they are to do? The business plan is not usually circulated in its complete form, not least because there is too much in it. Rather the plan is used to set targets for staff or for different departments and a summary is created to explain what is going on and what you want them to do.

Empowerment

The plan, once communicated, can prove to be a powerful motivator. It makes staff feel more involved, more confident and therefore more inclined to take personal responsibility and to take personal (rather than business) risks. Above all, staff know what they must do to contribute to achieving the plan – and may be able to put forward ideas, within the context of the plan.

Planning is not budgeting

Avoid tying planning to the budget cycle. Because the budget is inevitably done first, there are no new ideas contained in the section on the plan, which becomes simply a mathematical exercise. The plan is arrived at by taking the numbers from the budget and extending them by two or three years: 5 per cent per annum is added for extra sales, 4 per cent for staff costs, a 2 per cent per annum saving on energy, etc. Finally a budget commentary is added. All the benefits of the planning process, outlined above, are missed. There are no new ideas, there is no vision and the resulting document is not suitable for communication.

'How, then, do we see where our organization may be in three years' time?' you ask:

- Separate the budgeting from the planning. The plan comes first
  – because the budget for the forthcoming year should be seen as
  evaluating the first year of the plan – in some detail.

- Therefore you start with a strategy, through the planning process you test and develop a means of achieving this strategy, and that helps you create individual and department goals.

- Then you produce a financial forecast that evaluates the plan through its projected financial effects. This is probably done in summary form – don't go into the same detail as in a budget.

- Since the plan comes first, when the time comes to do the budget the figures may change and the plan figures may need to be re-evaluated. This should not be seen as a problem. The plan is about setting goals, specifying actions, etc and it would be strange if the budget produced such radically different results that these broad directions needed to be reconsidered. It should be seen as quite acceptable to update the numbers in the plan from time to time during the year, if necessary.

It takes only a few short paragraphs to state this but there is almost no advice on the planning process that is more important. You, or your colleagues, may feel that two processes of sitting around and discussing the future represents too great a diversion of management time from their main tasks. While you may appear to save time by combining budgeting and planning, since the result is actually a waste of time, you have saved nothing.

The benefits of planning are so great that it is the very essence of what management is about, so don't begrudge the time spent on it. Since it involves people being asked to come up with proposed actions to meet goals, is this not what you expect a manager or a director to be doing anyway?

The process does not have to be time-consuming and bureaucratic. One suggestion: get one person to coordinate the plan. Have one or two meetings of key people to thrash through the broad ideas and then get the coordinator to put together a first draft plan. Get initial responses from those key people without a meeting and then use a final meeting to reconcile any disagreements. This suggestion may not suit your circumstances but the point is that you can organize to avoid an excessive drain on scarce time. The right answer for you will depend upon your organization. But never blame 'planning'; excessive bureaucracy is your fault.

Non-traditional plans

The traditional business plan seeks to serve each of the purposes listed at the start of this chapter, though organizations may not always use them in that way. For example, many do not disseminate their business plan throughout the organization, therefore not fulfilling the plan's potential as a method of communication.

The traditional business plan provides a means of rigorously analysing intended strategies and systematically programming and codifying them before translating them into action plans and budgets. This type of plan generally also draws heavily on financial modelling so that the intended strategies and the various 'what ifs' can be costed and financial projections and cash flows can be analysed and planned.

This traditional model suffers from several drawbacks:

- It tends to be heavily analytical. It is written in the language of accountants and contains masses of figures that may make it hard for non-accountants to understand or identify with.

- It relies mainly on hard data. The 'soft', subjective, hard to define information about a business, which is missing, may be the most crucial to business success.

- It is often inflexible. Within weeks of its production, events in the 'real world' may have rendered it out of date and redundant.

- Finally, because it is by definition a large and detailed document, it is frequently put on a shelf, never to be referred to again.

That is not to say that a traditional, all-singing, all-dancing model is never a valuable and important process. It certainly can be – but, unless you wish to approach financial institutions for more capital, it tends to suit what Henry Mintzberg in *The Rise and Fall of Strategic Planning* describes as the 'Machine Organization – the classic bureaucracy'.

If it is to be truly useful the business plan must focus on:

- setting objectives for particular individuals and departments;

- specifying actions to be taken by particular individuals and departments;
- providing a vision to motivate and to guide decision making.

Strategic vision and action

The corporate vision: soft data and hard data

Some companies have written mission statements and statements of corporate values. At their best, these encapsulate a vision of where the company aspires to go, what it is trying to do, how it will be achieved and why this company is different. At their worst, they are meaningless drivel.

What is truly important is not the written statement but the vision for the company. Entrepreneurs will frequently hold this in their heads. It will be their inspiration. It will encapsulate something unique about the business and will guide decisions and actions. For all types of organization, it can be an enormously powerful motivator to management and staff who understand and share the vision and are enthused by it.

Customers will frequently recognize that the product or service that is guided by a vision is different from the offering of competitors, even if they have not read a detailed mission statement. The 'information' that makes up the vision for a business is not the analytical, numerical or 'hard data'. Whilst hard data (that is, figures, statistics, numerical market research, etc) are useful and should be collected and included where possible, these can leave just as large a margin for error in interpretation as soft data. The vision is primarily made up of and based on this soft data. Soft data comprises the views, opinions and perceptions of the people who work in the business, as well as the perceptions of customers and suppliers. It can be argued that soft data is more reliable than hard data and a business plan should certainly contain as much soft data as possible. Many studies show that the best strategic management decisions are made intuitively rather than analytically, though analysis certainly has its place too.

Having clear statements of vision, mission and values is an excellent means of communication with staff. If they understand that, say, excellent customer service is central to the beliefs of the organization then they are enabled to make better decisions; they will act in a way that is both compatible with the route mapped out for the organization and will further the achievement of its objectives.

The same ideas relate to the use of a customer charter; this should communicate with staff as well as with customers. The staff must understand and be committed to what they are expected to deliver (and how). They must be enthused by it rather than seeing it as a dull formula to be passed by 10 times a day and ignored.

Example: customer charter of Maher the Bookseller

We aim to offer our customers a superior service through better choice, better value and friendly, helpful staff. We will carry a wider range of books than any other local store. We will normally deliver any book that is not in stock within 48 hours. Our prices will often be lower than other local stores – and we will refund the difference if they are not. We will exchange or refund any purchase that is, for any reason, unsatisfactory.

Maher the Bookseller is an independent business that cares about its customers and what they think. If you have any comments to make please do speak to the manager or write to me.

The customer charter shown above is not only a series of promises to customers but is also a very clear statement to staff and to business partners of what the team they belong to is dedicated to deliver. The individual promises are very specific: it is clear if they have been met. This meets two of the fundamental criteria for a statement that is worthwhile. It has limited objectives, which is also characteristic of worthwhile customer charters, mission statements, etc; one cannot achieve everything in such a short space. It is displayed in the company's shops and so it is primarily communicating with customers; there is little about the overall vision of the business beyond the simple service concept, and there is nothing of the bargain between staff and owners, nor of how staff will be empowered to deliver the ideal of excellent service.

What sort of ideas make up a useful mission statement or corporate vision? Apple Computer's vision of making computers easy to use has clearly influenced every decision of the company as well as other computer makers throughout the world, albeit that it has taken many years for those others to achieve similar levels of simplicity and 'ease of use'.

The McDonald's hamburger chain has not always lived up to its aims for uniform high quality, bright, cheerful and clean surroundings, good quality food at a low price and fast service. But the whole business is clearly influenced and directed by such ideas.

However, it is very hard to define what is effective beyond the three characteristics that the statement must:

- be clear and simple;
- have limited objectives;
- be specific rather than general.

Remembering that planning is about actions and changing behaviours, note the sequence and interrelation of stages in the process:

1 Your plan starts with a vision – which may have been created through the involvement of a team of people.

2 The vision is communicated so that everyone is committed to it.

3 The vision is translated into goals and actions for achieving it.

4 This then becomes the 'agenda' for performance measurement, control and coordination and for continually reviewing the plan.

Creating strategy

It is very hard to write about how to go about creating strategy because it is nothing like a mechanical process. Although there are many business books that seem to be about developing strategy and a constant cycle of new approaches that come in and out of vogue, none of these books actually tells you how to have the ideas. After all the years and all the books there seems to be little improvement upon sitting around talking.

What works for one individual or organization may not work for others and may not work at a different time. Examples of possible routes to the idea generator include:

- taking a group of top executives to a hotel for a weekend, which may stimulate debate and ideas;
- using a skilled facilitator to help oil those rusted cogs;
- a series of short, internal meetings on the usual work premises may help in challenging ideas;
- involving more junior staff through departmental meetings may reveal unexpected depth of skill and resources.

These ideas are all about getting groups of people within an organization to produce new ideas, but what about stimulating individual thinking? For a small organization there may only be one person to create strategy and to plan. For them the stimulants may be:

- going on courses (eg short courses at business schools);
- finding someone to talk to (consultants, friends and chance acquaintances may stimulate thinking);
- reading business books (even books with which you disagree may stimulate thinking).

How, though, do you channel the ideas? As I have said above, heavily structured planning closes down ideas rather than stimulating them.

Exercise

Create and consider ideas by posing yourself questions:

1 What business are you in? For example, consider the British Airports Authority – is it in the business of transportation or of retail or both? Is it perhaps a property developer? Simply thinking about this issue leads on to other issues which, in turn, suggest a series of possible strategies.

2 What skills and strengths do you have? Could these take you in a new direction?

3 What trends are observable in your own or related markets? Can you foresee gradual or sudden changes that may give rise to opportunities for someone? What is happening overseas? What are your competitors doing that is innovative?

4 What threats can you reasonably foresee from: changes in your customers, in regulation, in technology, in cost structures, in the economy, etc?

5 Think about your customers. What unsatisfied needs do they have or may they have in future?

Through considering and discussing general questions, ideas are stimulated that can then be fed into the more traditional sort of planning process. When you are at the stage of creating ideas, don't criticize suggestions or the people who put them forward – however crazy they may seem. That discourages people from putting ideas forward. Have a rule that only positive and encouraging responses are allowed. Later, you can go through a process of questioning which may lead to ideas being discarded. Later, one takes an idea and forms a plan of how it might be pursued, which tests its practicability. As a result, many ideas will be abandoned but new strategies will emerge. Never make someone feel small because they have put forward a silly idea; their next one may be a treasure.

When you put together the team to work on a strategy always make sure it includes people with current front-line experience of dealing with customers, suppliers and operations. It is too easy for these matters to be handled by finance people and divisional directors who, whatever their previous experience, are now removed and distanced from these details. Critical insights demand current experience of these details even if greater experience and authority is also required to know what has been tried before and what impediments there may be to suggestions. Note also that just because something was tried before and did not work does not mean it may not work now.

Conduct action-oriented planning

A business plan that is drawn up to help to manage a business must result in actions. If nothing is done as a result of the plan then it is of no use and the time devoted to producing it has been wasted. It should not, therefore, just map out broad strategies and objectives. How do you ensure that a plan does not just sit on a shelf, gathering dust? There are four disciplines that lead to useful plans:

- establish goals and strategies;
- involve staff who must carry out the plan and win their commitment to the plan (see 'Involving staff – building the team');
- have clear actions specified and responsibilities defined;
- review progress at least once each year and be prepared to amend the plan or to deal with people who are not meeting their objectives.

The end result of this planning exercise must be a written document that sets goals for a business or activity and states what must be done to achieve those goals or targets. Ideally it will also state who must do what and by when. It may be that the process of producing the plan will be in two or more parts; after setting the broad objectives and strategy it may need a second phase to define detail and to specify precise actions. If the broad objectives are set at a senior level within an organization, it will usually be appropriate to involve those at a lower level. These people will then be involved in setting objectives for their own areas in order to carry out the overall plan.

One of the keys to such action-oriented planning is that the actions must be specific and measurable. You must be able to tell when they have been done and whether they have worked. Don't define actions that are so vague that it is impossible to tell when they have been done: improving customer contacts is no good as an objective – it must be improving customer contacts through x visits and y telephone conversations each month, resulting in z per cent increase in business. There is then a mechanism for person J to be responsible for making this happen and for the owner or the board or divisional manager or person G to review progress in six months.

That review must also result in actions. The results of such a review are seldom black or white; everything may be on target and nothing may need to be done. However, it is much more likely that some specified actions have not been carried out or some have not been successful. Indeed it may be that some targets have been over-achieved and that something must be done about that. The result of the review should be:

- finding out why actions have not been taken;
- doing things to ensure they are done in a timely manner;
- setting revised targets, actions and timing;
- revising the plan itself if appropriate.

However, there are some essential objectives that are intrinsically hard to measure. Consider the objective example below, extracted from a business plan formulated by Psion Software Plc. (Note that IIP stands for Investors in People, a UK government-sponsored personnel standard.)

Example

Goal: To improve communication and training

Responsibility: ....

Last revised: ....

What will this goal achieve?

- We will regularly review the needs and plan the training and development of everyone in the company.

- We will evaluate our training and development efforts and improve them continuously.

- We will improve our internal communications. This is especially important to employees based outside of... or... many of whom complain of not being tapped into the zeitgeist of... and this is even worse for employees working outside the UK.

- We will agree a common perception of where we as... are trying to go and everyone will know their own contribution to us getting there.

- The company will achieve IIP accreditation, which is a British professional standard for doing the above. This says something concrete and positive to current and future employees/customers and is a measurable goal.

How will we achieve this goal?

- We have appointed an IIP consultant... and she will work alongside our personnel department.

- She will begin by interviewing a representative selection of employees. From this will come an agreed action plan, to be followed by further surveys to test the improvement. When surveys indicate suitable improvement we apply for IIP.

- We will do more to ensure messages are getting through. We will check that messages are being properly communicated via Team Briefs and cascaded briefs, eg more management walkabouts and more listening. And we will be more responsive by getting back to people quickly, even if it is to say we do not yet have an answer.

How will we know we've achieved this goal?

- We will have achieved IIP.

This section of the plan sets a measurable goal – achievement of the Investors in People standard. Yet it also sets improvement in communications – how does one know this has been achieved? The answer is the use of employee attitude surveys. Other possible means of measuring these 'softer' factors include: exit interviews, discussion groups, use of external consultants. Even hard to define targets can be measured if you try.

Where are you starting from?

Think of a business plan as a route map of a journey. You are starting here and aiming to get to there. On the way there are many difficulties. The terrain and weather represent the conditions of the markets you trade in. It may be mountainous or hilly, there may be swamps and rivers. The competition is represented by fierce monsters that will try to eat you. To complicate matters they may move around and change shape just like real competitors. Changing conditions are represented by storms, earthquakes and floods. On your journey there may be friends who can be your allies and help you deal with some of these problems. They may help you across ravines or provide boats over rivers.

Your skills and abilities are represented by where you start from, by your fitness, agility and strength and by things you carry with you on your journey. So you may be able to dodge some monsters, beat down others with weapons you have brought or use ropes you carry to climb down a cliff face.

Pursuing this metaphor, we have an answer for all those people who claim they are too busy to take part in time-wasting planning. We are all too busy: we all have too much to do. But imagine these people as struggling through a swamp, carrying a huge weight ('their workload') on their backs. It is so heavy that they are bent double and they inch along through the mud looking down at their feet. Of course, if they made the effort to look up, they might have to stop for a moment and it would be a strain to straighten up. However, if they did so, they might spot the slow-moving herd of buffalo moving their way – which is going to trample them into a pulp. Or they might see the road, only a few paces away, that would make their journey so much easier. Using planning, like using a route map on a journey, is essential to finding your way.

There are three major differences between the journey of a business plan and a normal physical journey:

1 Markets, competitors, technology, customers, government regulations, etc, may change frequently and radically, although most ordinary journeys are over pretty static terrain.

2 Whereas the road map you buy in a shop is fairly clear, the route map of this business plan journey may well be quite unclear in places; sadly you can't see all the obstacles or enemies until you are right on top of them.

3 Your destination may change between different versions of a business plan as conditions change and you re-evaluate your situation.

Now it seems obvious where you are starting from and what your skills are but these things are seldom as obvious as they seem. Few business plans really delve into these things honestly. SWOT analysis, which is about listing Strengths, Weaknesses, Opportunities and Threats, is now standard in many plans. However, the way it is done usually makes it a complete waste of time. It is usually about 'saluting the flag' and stating the obvious. When people write down as strengths that they are 'market leaders' or that they are 'the most entrepreneurial team' around, are they being honest and truthful? Well, sometimes they are but mostly they are trying to delude themselves or their superiors. The clear sign of this is the use of vague generalities, which are difficult to test.

However, overleaf is an example of a statement of strengths and weaknesses compiled for a retail chain in the early 1990s. It suffers some weaknesses, but is not bad.

Strengths

- the leading specialist brand in the market;
- national presence although biased towards London;
- well known and well regarded amongst book buyers;
- a relatively aggressive position in terms of price, promotion and value;
- strong representation among the main target demographic groups;
- attractive and well laid out stores;
- potentially effective and helpful staff;
- an embryonic mailing list and account card system.

Weaknesses

- inability to assess full marketing performance because of lack of MIS (management information system);
- a very diverse mix of stores, with the inability to give one message;
- stores possibly too clinical in character;
- more work to be done about the staff attitude, and effective point of sale messages;
- overall 'promiscuity' of customers.

The assessment shown above is fairly honest and covers most of the weaknesses. Where it fails is only in not carrying through – some but not all of the points are addressed in the plan. The point of assessing strengths and weaknesses, opportunities and threats has to be as a starting point for saying what will be done about them. Never state a weakness and then omit to say what will be done about it, even if you have to say that the problem is relatively minor and there is nothing that can be done. Try not to state strengths without thinking about how to exploit them even more effectively. The SWOT analysis is not just an academic exercise – you do it to try to assess the likelihood of success of your plans and to stimulate new ideas. SWOT analysis should lead to actions.

Always start an internal business plan by writing sections on the markets you are involved in and on your own strengths and weaknesses. But how do you write an honest assessment of where you are? As far as possible, use quantifiable statements; for example, you will not find yourself claiming market leadership if you write that your main competitor has a 60 per cent market share. You may assert that you are potentially leaders in a particular niche of a market and, if you define this niche and write some evidence to support this view, you will both avoid deluding yourself and define some elements of your strategy.

A useful technique is to compare yourself with competitors and potential competitors on a grid. For example:

	Financial strength	Product range	Product quality	Service
Ourselves	B	A	B	A–
Competitor A	A	C–	B	A
Competitor B	C	C–	B	B

You will best know the appropriate measures to use. Which are really significant? Choose the significant ones and ignore the rest. Once you have drawn a grid like this you will find it a lot easier to describe where you are at present.

Another technique is to start from how others see you. You may use outside consultants, students doing a project, new or junior members of your team. You may use a review of the trade press or a questionnaire given to customers. Some organizations use climate surveys among their own staff to test morale and to discover how their own staff see them. This can only be successful if an outside consultant is used so that staff are assured of anonymity.

If you are not honest, then your plan will be useless: you may be setting unachievable objectives and your route map starts at the wrong place. After a short distance you may find that one of those monsters, whom you asserted was weak and feeble, comes along and knocks you down.

Two of the major differences from a real map were mentioned above: things changing and things being unclear. There are only two ways of dealing with these problems: continual research and maintaining flexibility. For a small organization, research may seem expensive but simple techniques like constantly reviewing the trade press and considering the implications of the news may suffice. Obtaining your competitors' catalogues and discussing needs and wants with your customers may similarly be relatively cheap and may produce better information than expensively commissioned research. Smaller organizations ought to be more flexible than giant competitors and may be able to react more quickly – but don't be too arrogant and assume that this is so: there are big, flexible organizations too.

Planning for people

Involving staff – building the team

If the purpose of the plan is to guide management action (and even perhaps if it is to raise money) then the plan needs:

1 *Ownership* by all of those who are required to carry it out. If people don't believe in a plan then they will not make it happen. At best, they will give acquiescence but will withhold enthusiasm and at worst they will sabotage it. They won't believe in a plan:

- that is imposed from above;
- if they are not consulted in its formation;

- if they disagree with targets, proposed actions to meet targets, or anything.

But ownership means it is *their* plan and ownership leads to…

2 *Commitment*, because they want to make it succeed and this leads to enthusiasm and to:

- hard work – which results in people achieving the unachievable;
- feedback – when management find out valuable information about how their business works from their staff;
- ideas – when people come up with ideas that assist the achievement of the plan;
- customer service – staff who are committed will deliver better customer service;
- communication – with superiors, subordinates, customers and suppliers improves when staff are committed to what they are doing.

Creating the future through your staff

There is a strong case for most business plans to include consideration of issues of skills and manpower. For most of us, our staff provide us with the skills and motivated effort that will ensure success, which means that the plan must consider what skills are needed to achieve the business goals set out elsewhere in the plan. To get them there is a need to have a human resources plan to set out how you will recruit, develop and retain the right staff. Don't forget staff development in this mix because that has several important aspects. People join and stay with companies not just because of the rate of pay but also because they see the experience – including training – will advance their career. Staff development comes in many guises and does not have to mean spending money on training courses, though that may be an appropriate option.

For example, a significant part of the development of skills arises from giving staff relevant experience at work. Supervisory skills will be developed by giving them supervisory experience, perhaps in conjunction with some coaching from someone within the business. In turn, developing people's coaching skills has an immediate payback through enabling them to bring on other work colleagues and will also make them better managers. Where learning is required outside the organization there are many ways to do this, from allowing someone flexible working time or time off to study to paying for them to attend college or use distance learning. Depending upon the size of an organization it may be appropriate to have training provided in-house.

It is often expensive and ineffective to address many HR issues in a piecemeal and disjointed way. For example, there are sometimes fashions in this area of management as in many others and so perhaps an employee opinion survey will be the current fashion. The HR director or manager may put this forward as an excellent and forward-looking thing to do in the organization. What I argue is that this is only a tool not an end in itself. Go back a step and formulate an integrated human resource strategy that works as a whole to support the business strategy. An employee opinion survey may well form a part of this but don't introduce initiatives because they seem a good idea on their own: always pursue initiatives because they are part of a bigger plan and promote achievement of the business goals.

Employee opinion surveys have shown that personal development opportunities are very important to people in choosing employers and in staying with them, so money invested in this has a clear payback. Just as clearly some individual staff will inevitably leave before giving their organizations a payback, nonetheless, overall the benefit is proven. Providing a career path and rewarding staff who improve their worth to you is important in the retention process.

Clearly a business plan does not require a person-by-person analysis but the broad needs, objectives and systems to achieve them should be clearly set out, together with estimated costs and, ideally, a statement of benefits. If in-house development will save a substantial sum in recruitment costs then it is appropriate to estimate this.

Practicalities

Tips for producing and using the business plan

The following tips may be particularly helpful for internal business plans:

1 Before starting work on any planning, the people involved should agree clearly who the resulting document is for and what it is for (who and why).

2 The plan should be clear and easy to read. It does not need to be a literary masterpiece, neither does it need to be a detailed, flawless piece of work.

3 The development of the plan must have commitment, support and involvement at a senior level for large organizations but should include at least the next management level, if not the next two levels, depending on the size of the organization. It is often appropriate for people with direct and everyday customer contact to be involved in the planning team at the very beginning.

4 Once the plan has been developed, it should be dated and rapidly communicated. It is a snapshot in time. Organizations and individuals move on and change fast: it is not worth getting too concerned about continually changing the plan, or worse still to delay communicating it because something is about to happen. The plan should be treated as a snapshot in time and therefore as a starting point for getting new things done and for getting more things done.

Many people do, however, find that a business plan is a useful reference document and they find it helpful to keep it updated. This should, of course, be encouraged but not enforced as it will depend on the style of the individual.

5 Key business objectives should be taken out of the plan and translated into short-term action plans which should be sent up and down the organization.

6 Training and development plans should be drawn up from these key business objectives.

7 Options, or what-ifs, should be considered. This can only cover a few scenarios or the plan would take years to produce. However, this approach keeps the plan flexible and it remains useful even when one of those what-ifs happens, which would have invalidated a rigid plan.

If the plan is to be flexible it should concentrate on setting objectives and upon outlining broad strategies for getting there. The more detailed it is, the more quickly that detail will become outdated – objectives, on the other hand, age more slowly.

8 Use of consultants to help in planning can be helpful when individuals and organizations are not practised in the art of producing them. However, it is crucial that outside assistance is used to facilitate the production of the plan – not to write it. The managers must feel a sense of ownership of the plan and therefore commitment to it. If other people write the plan then it is their plan, particularly when things go wrong.

9 Key business and training and development objectives derived from the plan should be used in the performance management, or performance appraisal, programme.

Adapting to reality

Yes, but it doesn't turn out like you planned. Well, that's reality, things seldom do turn out quite like we plan.

When we set up a new retail business we had lots of excellent ideas for staff training and for providing customer information. We were experienced in the business and we knew they were good ideas; they would radically improve staff service and customer satisfaction. However, we were not experienced in setting up a new business and did not realize how few hours there are in a day, nor how much there is to do nor how tired you get. Many great ideas had to wait for a second phase of development when we hoped to have more staff to share the workload.

We learnt two important lessons that apply even to the most experienced managers: sometimes you get it wrong, and an effective business plan is not meant to relate to a static world.

The writers accept that the plan must adapt to the objectives that turn out to be unrealistic, to the new and unforeseen product on the market or the new competitor. The plan, to be useful, must be reviewed. These reviews must not take place so frequently that people who are involved turn off from the whole process, but often enough to ensure that the plan remains relevant. The appropriate timing will depend upon circumstances; more frequently for a new business or a rapidly changing market or a larger company – where informal discussion and amendment may be more difficult because more people would have to be involved than in a smaller company.

Some companies and other organizations undertake annual planning rounds, often as part of the budgeting process. It is a *very* bad idea to confuse the two. The budgeting process is about the short term and about setting financial goals and forecasts in order to control an organization. It is fundamentally a numbers-driven process. Internal business plans are about reviewing goals and implementing strategies; they should be about ideas, and while numbers are important, they should follow on from the ideas and illustrate the implications and results of the plan.

When planning is conducted as an annual chore the document normally sits on a shelf for a year and the next plan may be constructed with no more than a cursory glance at the previous one. It is just a mechanical process forced on management by the boss head office and a bit of a waste of time. The plan must be reviewed during the year if it is to be of any practical use and normal monthly reporting should comment upon progress against the plan. The plan must be in your mind all the time as a vision of where you are trying to get to and how you expect to get there: it should be an integral part of managing an organization.

The steps to take to review the plan should be:

- How have things progressed compared with the plan?
- What went wrong (and what went right)?

- Why did things go wrong or right?
- What can be done to address failure and reinforce success?
- Have your views of the future changed?
- Are the objectives and strategy still valid?
- Reset objectives and strategy for the organization.
- Reset individual goals and/or timing.

As with the initial plan, it remains essential that those who must implement the plan are involved in its review and committed to the targets and actions required from them.

Even when circumstances have changed, don't change your final objectives too frequently, not unless it really is necessary. Having set up our retail business we soon found that a competitor, which we had dismissed as unimportant, grew by 50 per cent per annum over three years to become a serious force in the market and floated on the stock exchange, raising more money for continued future growth. Would their growth squeeze out our opportunities? We decided that they had validated our own growth model through following similar strategies and had demonstrated the viability of the sort of sites we were pursuing, of which there were many available for both of us.

Therefore, even bad news may not require a total rethink.

The dead hand of corporate politics

One of the major factors blocking success in any organization is internal rivalry and conflict. It can start in very small organizations as well as big ones. You only need two people to start an argument. It arises particularly where resources are limited and you have to fight for your share. Therefore it may not be surprising that hospitals, research organizations and universities often come up as examples of this tendency. It also arises where organizations have adopted a feudal culture, with departmental 'barons' fighting for power and influence and, in the long term, career advancement. In the 1980s, many merchant banks were torn apart by these cultural conflicts, which divert energy away from the real business. It may be argued that it was this cultural problem, above all others, that led to the lack of success and profitability of particular organizations.

This is not the place to address in detail this complex problem of internal politics. It is an issue of organizational culture and the requirements for changing it take time and can be very difficult to achieve.

The culture of the organization must be that the goals of the whole organization are paramount and not those of a department or section – this is one of the benefits of producing a 'vision' that unites and inspires all staff. Support for this must come from the top. This is a necessary but not sufficient requirement for cultural change. You won't get anywhere without the backing of the leadership but even good leaders can struggle to change organizational culture – especially in large organizations.

But we must consider how it impacts upon business planning. The main problems are:

- avoiding the issues;
- sabotaging the plan;
- promising the leader what he/she wants.

Example

A large US-based multinational 'A' was confronted with serious strategic issues. As number two in a technology-dominated market operating worldwide, they were a long way behind the leader, which was nearly three times the size and far more profitable. There was another, more specialist competitor that had come from nowhere only a few years previously and was growing very fast. Not only was it now two-thirds the size but it had captured dominance of the most profitable market segments. By contrast, 'A' was stagnating, was dominated by salesmen and had technology that was rapidly becoming outdated. The major cause of problems was that its US parent had treated this business as a generator of cash and had under-invested over many years.

Faced with large problems, Joe, the head of the UK end of the business, decided to draw up a strategic plan, which was also required for his objective of attaining the Investors in People standard. However, he insisted upon getting the individual regional divisions and head office departments to draw up their own plans for consolidation in an overall plan. A consultant was engaged to carry out this consolidation but Joe was not prepared for the consultant to challenge or question, only to provide guidance notes.

The result was a series of disconnected plans produced by people who had no experience of planning, which simply did not address the key issues of the business or of their parts of it.

Sabotage is not a simple problem; one or more individuals seek to misdirect the planning process for their own ends. However, this can occur through: 1) Making it difficult for any result to emerge from the process. A key individual may miss meetings, demand further study of particular issues, decline to cooperate, etc. 2) Misdirecting the process. One or more individuals may seek to get their own position improved by pushing for their interests, notwithstanding the detriment to the organization.

The only solution is the use of force to remove obstructive people and to oblige any key individuals to cooperate and to discipline them if necessary.

Promising the leader what they want can be the most destructive of all impediments to successful planning. The other political problems that have been mentioned can be overcome through strong leadership, but if the leader of an organization is involved in the self-deception, there is no hope.

X was a public company that had run into financial problems and, under pressure from institutional shareholders, had brought in consultants and appointed a new chief executive from outside the company. This man, Ted, believed himself to be a 'marketing' man. He challenged the board of one of the subsidiary companies to come up with a plan to increase sales by 10 million. His explanation was that sales and profits were simply too low in relation to the capital invested in the business.

Now, while I agree that managers must be challenged, from time to time, to think radically and to review the whole way they do things, this demand had a very simple consequence. The marketing director drew up a plan which proposed a greatly increased advertising spend that would achieve the sales increase – simple. In other circumstances a chief executive might be expected to question the plan and to ask what evidence there was to suggest that higher sales would result from the higher spend. However, Ted was under pressure to show that he was doing something. Maybe he was out of his depth and was desperately searching for any solution that might work. So the spend was authorized, the budgets revised and... sales did not increase. I doubt that the marketing director who put forward the plan was surprised.

How do we deal with the dead hand of internal politics? Successful organizations operate as a team whose focus is achieving success targets for the whole organization. Endemic conflict must be dispersed through changing the culture within afflicted organizations. The simple, short-term, answers are:

- Planning only works properly where there is commitment from the top both to the process and to the results.

- Encourage a climate of questioning and challenging the results, so that a useful end is achieved.

- The planning process is not primarily for forming strategy but for implementing strategy.

I was involved in the planning cycle of a large public company that had just passed through a traumatic experience. It had taken over another company in a hotly contested bid, which resulted in many people losing their jobs or their status and there were many bruised people in the organization.

Almost everything was wrong with the planning process. To start with, it was done as a continuation of the budget: it was not about pursuing new ideas or communicating – it was merely an enormous effort devoted to extending the budget forecasts for three years. However, the most extraordinary aspect was that there was no questioning or challenging of the divisional plans – which were of a remarkably poor standard. The chairman explained that it was too sensitive to quiz directors – particularly in view of the recent takeover – although I was invited to write a note on each plan for the chairman to use as a briefing paper for an informal chat with each divisional director. I am not sure these were ever used.

The plans were never improved or reconsidered and, in a remarkably short time, the company was bankrupt. Could an improved planning process have averted disaster? Maybe not. But the attitude of avoiding difficult questions and of using planning as part of a political process was indicative of a deeper malaise that sought to avoid uncomfortable thoughts. It ensured that the hours devoted to planning were wasted time that could have been better spent.

Summary points

- Business planning is not budgeting. Planning should be about ideas, strategies and direction, while budgeting is about numbers and targets and detail.

- Good business plans include 'soft information' such as vision and values and insight.

- The plan must guide actions: what you (and others) will do as a result.

And two more points:

- Reality will prove different from the plan, so adapt the plan to new circumstances.

- To avoid internal politics the process must be driven from the top of the organization, which must not tolerate politicking.

14
Bidding for business

The business plan is frequently used for bidding or tendering for contracts, for funding and for properties. The recipient of the plan may be a government department, a landlord, the purchasing department of a large organization, etc. The format of these plans is much the same as any other plan because you are still telling a story about the background of your organization, what it can do and how it will achieve benefits for the readers; however, there are some important differences too.

These plans are much shorter and more focused on particular issues. They are often produced in response to an 'invitation to tender'. While the readers may wish to know the background to your organization, they particularly need specific questions answered. They may have many documents like yours to read and therefore they want each to be short. Don't write pages of information that is irrelevant to these readers. For example, they may know all about the market – so you need only include in your plan any different interpretation or new data that may allow you to demonstrate your expertise. This may be particularly important when the body letting a tender will benefit from your ability to operate more effectively than your rivals, for example by creating higher sales when you will pay a turnover-related rent.

You may be given a format to use in your reply to a tender. This helps the recipients to compare one plan against another with the minimum of effort. Even if they don't specify a precise format, their 'invitation to tender' may refer to particular questions they want addressed: read their document carefully in order to be sure you answer each of these questions.

> *Fort is a large arts complex in a major city. It operates a theatre, concert hall, art gallery and cinema on the same site. It was seeking a new operator for its gift shop. It naturally wanted to make as much money as possible but its stated objectives did not mention money at all. They were:*
>
> - *to create retail outlets that reflect the centre's range of activities and art forms;*
>
> - *to create retail outlets that cater to all the centre's patrons and resident organizations;*
>
> - *to offer keen pricing and a clear marketing plan.*

It is usually very important to strike a rapport with the key staff within the organization seeking bids in order to:

- understand their true priorities;

- understand who will recommend the winner and know what their priorities are;

- find out if there are any important things you should know that are not specified in the tender document.

As illustrated above, there may be non-financial objectives which must be met. The plan must address these issues very clearly at the front of the document.

> *Fort's document inviting tenders included the following statements:*
>
> - *The contract period may be three or five years, depending upon the size of your capital investment: allow for both options in your proposal.*
>
> - *A minimum guaranteed rent will be expected.*
>
> - *Tenders should state how the centre will benefit from a change in retail operator.*
>
> - *The details of the stock range should be set out.*

The difficulty for the writer of the business plan is to be sure that these points are addressed very clearly while retaining the narrative flow of the 'story'. The technique for resolving this should be to write the plan as you feel illustrates your story and then to review it against each of the key points raised in the briefing document and whatever else you have learnt in conversation. Think carefully about what else you can offer that is not specified in any invitation to tender, so that you can differentiate your response from all those others.

> One company, which was seeking retail sites for its expansion programme, produced a professionally printed background document about themselves. Landlords of retail schemes often want to secure tenants who will bring something different in terms of class or design to their developments. Flair may not be enough to outweigh a high or secure rent but it may sway the balance where everything else is equal. While the carefully crafted words contained in the document were important, the colour photographs and the striking design conveyed, even more strongly, something of the spirit and flair of the company: it certainly resulted in the recipients remembering the sender and probably helped procure sites that might otherwise have slipped to someone else.

Although you might not immediately think of the document outlined above as a business plan, almost all the ideas were taken directly from the business plan of the organization – only the numbers were omitted.

Summary points

- Find out what the potential business partner wants.
- Focus the document on those needs.
- Cut out irrelevant detail.

APPENDICES

Appendix 1
The confidentiality letter

This letter is given as an illustration only. It may not meet the reader's needs and may prove unenforceable. The author accepts no responsibility in relation to anyone using it. The reader who needs an actual confidentiality letter should take professional advice.

Dear Sir or Madam,

The information contained in the Information Memorandum ('The Information') to be sent to you is the property of John Smith and is commercially valuable. By signing this letter XXX acknowledges this and undertakes:

1 *Not to use the information for its own commercial purposes.* Not to establish or acquire a business in the same trade or approach or enter into commercial negotiations with any staff, customers or suppliers of John Smith for a period of 12 months following the date of this letter.

2 To keep the information confidential. To take all reasonable care to avoid disclosing The Information in whole or in part either directly or indirectly to anyone except its own staff and professional advisers in order for them to work on the proposed acquisition of John Smith. It undertakes only to disclose the whole or part of The Information after its staff or professional advisers have been bound to the undertakings to John Smith on the same terms as this letter.

3 Not to make any copies of the information without permission and on the request of John Smith to return the documents

and to destroy any copies or extracts that may have been taken or made.

The signatory acknowledges that the appropriate recourse for any breaches of this undertaking comprises injunctive relief in addition to damages.

XXX indemnifies John Smith for any actions, claims, costs, expenses, liabilities, losses or payments arising from the breach of this undertaking by itself or any employee or professional adviser.

The terms of this letter do not apply to information that is already in the public domain or becomes so, other than through a breach of this undertaking.

The signatories agree that this undertaking shall be governed by English Law.

Yours faithfully,

John Smith   Date............................

  Agreed by,

Jim Jones for XXX   Date............................

Appendix 2
Reconciling profit and cash flow

The chart below illustrates how the profit and cash flow should reconcile in a simple business. It may look like a pretty scary mass of numbers to someone who is not used to a cash flow but let me explain…

There are 12 columns showing the cash flows in each month of this business's financial year – which happens to run from January to December. Businesses actually have all sorts of financial years ending in virtually any month. The thirteenth column totals the months and shows the cash flows for the year. The next column shows the profit and loss account for comparison, and the final column shows differences between the year's cash and profit columns.

The first question is: why are sales different in the cash and profit columns? It is because of credit: some of the sales achieved in any month are actually paid for in the following month. Similarly, the suppliers are paid in the following month and so there is a difference here too. These two differences show up in the entries for debtors and creditors in the balance sheet of the business under a section called working capital. I have simplified this business – there is no change in the levels of stock held during the year nor any timing differences in property, staff costs or other costs. In a real business there would be differences that would all show up in changes in the working capital.

Towards the bottom of the chart are items such as investment in new computers, a loan taken out to finance those computers and taxes paid. The first two don't show up in the profit and loss account, although they are real cash items, because they are part of the fixed assets and financing of the business, not part of its profit. The third item, taxes, would normally be shown in the profit and loss account. I have not shown them there in order to try to simplify the chart at the risk of causing confusion. I have cut off the P&L before the tax level because taxes are usually paid on the

	Jan	Feb	Mar	Apr	May	Jun	Jul	Aug	Sep	Oct	Nov	Dec	Year	Profit and loss account	Difference cash flow: profit
CASH FROM TRADING															
Sales	70	65	75	80	80	70	85	85	95	110	125	175	1,115	1,130	15
Cost of sales	−79	−32	−29	−34	−36	−36	−32	−38	−38	−43	−50	−56	−502	509	−7
														45%	
Gross profit														622	
Staff costs	−14	−14	−14	−14	−14	−14	−14	−14	−14	−14	−14	−14	−170	170	0
Property costs	−7	−7	−28	−7	−7	−28	−7	−7	−28	−7	−7	−28	−170	170	0
Other overheads	−6	−6	−6	−6	−6	−6	−6	−6	−6	−6	−6	−6	−68	68	0
Interest paid			−4			−7			−6			−2	−19	19	
CASH FROM TRADING	**−36**	**7**	**−6**	**19**	**17**	**−21**	**27**	**20**	**3**	**40**	**49**	**69**	**187**	196	
OTHER CASH FLOWS															
New computer investment							−40						−40		
New loan for computers								30					30		
Taxes						−50							−50		
Total cash	**−36**	**7**	**−6**	**19**	**17**	**−71**	**−13**	**50**	**3**	**40**	**49**	**69**	**127**		
Depreciation														84	
Profit before tax														112	

previous year's profits and so there would be a difference between the P&L tax item and the cash flow tax item.

But let us reconcile the two 'Year' columns:

Profit	112
Add back depreciation	84
	196
Adjust for capital and financing	–60
	136
Adjust for working capital	–8
	128

But this adjusted total is 128, although the cash flow column shows 127, why? The answer is that there will often be rounding errors unless you show numbers to several decimal points. I believe it is unhelpful to show excessive apparent accuracy and would rather be left with a rounding error. Too many numbers creates confusion rather than enlightenment and pretends at a level of accuracy that is seldom achieved.

Appendix 3
The cash forecast

Two big secrets: cash forecasting is not hard and it does not necessarily call for a qualified accountant. There, the secret's out.

Cash forecasting is especially important if your business is short of cash or if times are tough. It matters because finding yourself with no money to pay suppliers, taxes or employees, even if only for a few days, has serious consequences. You may be unable to trade, your suppliers may refuse to supply or may withdraw credit, utilities may be cut off, bailiffs may take your goods, bankers may withdraw your facilities and, in the worst case, your business may be declared insolvent.

If you want to produce a cash forecast then this template describes how to do it. The easiest way is on a spreadsheet but it is perfectly possible to draw lines on a piece of paper and use a pencil and a calculator. A pencil is better than a pen because there are bound to be changes and rubbing out.

What will you need?

You need: a cautious sales forecast; details of debts owed to you, your business bank statements for the past year; details from your accounting system of both what invoices are due to be paid and when and also what your customers are due to pay you and when; your bank balance as at last night.

A word about the forecast. Produce your best guess of what sales you will achieve, when you will achieve them and, really important, when you will be paid for them. Be cautious but not ridiculously cautious. If businesses forecast only the very worst scenario then most would be bankrupt.

Be cautious, when looking at monies payable to you; think of any disputes you have outstanding and any customers who are late payers. If you are a retailer, remember that credit card companies pay into your bank account, less their commission, several days after the sale is made.

Your bank statements tell you when standing orders and direct debits are payable and how much they usually are. Don't forget things like bank interest or charges.

What the forecast looks like

The forecast comes in two sections: incoming cash and outgoing cash (shown as a minus number). For example:

	Period 1	**Period 2**	**Period 3**
Sales	10	20	30
Costs	−5	−25	−15
Net inflow/outflow	5	−5	15
Opening bank balance	5	10	5
Closing bank balance	10	5	20

The flows of cash are worked out for periods that can be a year, a quarter, a month or even a day. Why would you want a daily cash forecast? If you exceed your overdraft limit – even by a small amount – for just a day, the bank may refuse to honour your payments. And a single occasion where that happens may lead them to re-examine and reconsider any facilities you have. It does you no good that you will have plenty of cash at the end of next month or at the end of next week if you are short of cash in the middle of next week. Actually it may do some good if you can convince the bank manager and persuade the bank to give you a temporary increase in facilities... which just proves how critical the cash forecast is.

I have shown just a line for sales and a line for costs. This is a simplification, you will want to put more detail than that. How much detail depends upon how complicated your business is and how accurate you need to be. I have always grouped the costs into categories and have generally shown them supplier-by-supplier. Don't forget taxes and professional fees and utility bills, subscription fees and carriage costs. What matters will be different for each business. If long lists are too complex for a single spreadsheet you can always put them on another spreadsheet and transfer the period totals to the main summary spreadsheet. Exactly the same thinking applies to sales. So you might have:

	Period 1	Period 2	Period 3
SALES			
Customer 1	10	10	10
Customer 2	0	10	10
Customer 3	5	0	10
Total	**15**	**20**	**30**
COSTS			
Stock purchases	−3	−5	−7
Wages etc	−5	−5	−5
Property costs		−10	
Overhead costs	−2	−3	−3
VAT and other taxes		−2	
Total	**−10**	**−25**	**−15**
Net inflow/outflow	5	−5	15
Opening bank balance	5	10	5
Closing bank balance	10	5	20

The sales forecast

The main driver of the cash forecast is the sales forecast which you then adjust for when you expect to be paid. You may sell on 30, 60 or even 90 days' credit. You may sell on credit but then use a factoring service to get some of the cash sooner. You must even think about bad debts and credit insurance. All these details must be thought through in the process of converting the sales forecast into a cash forecast. Remember that you may give different credit terms to different customers. This can seem complicated but actually it is just a matter of being disciplined – it takes time to list out the customers with their different sales forecasts and different payment terms – but is not difficult to convert one to the other – it is the original sales forecast that is hard.

	Period 1	Period 2	Period 3	Period 4	Period 5
SALES					
Customer A	10	10	5	10	20
Customer B	15	15	20	20	20
Customer C	20	10	20	25	25
Total	**45**	**35**	**45**	**55**	**65**
CASH					
Customer A (30 days)		10	10	5	10
Customer B (60 days)				15	20
Customer C (90 days)			15	20	10
Total	**0**	**10**	**25**	**40**	**40**

For illustration I have shown a 30-day account paying at the beginning of the following month. It is probably safest to assume you will pay your bills on time while your customers will pay a few days late. Trust me: some will pay late.

Check the forecast

How do you check your forecast? Maybe you have missed something important – a cost that had slipped your mind or you never thought of.

Look at past management accounts and budgets: do the categories of cost seem reasonable in comparison? Calculate the key ratios, if wage costs have always been around 33 per cent of sales income but your forecast shows 25 per cent then maybe you have made a mistake here.

What can I do?

Suppose that the forecast shows a period when the bank balance is a 35,000 overdraft but your facility is only 30,000.

First, recheck your assumptions. If you have made some broad estimates then look in fine detail and try to refine the figures. Let us suppose this makes no difference. Remember that this cash forecast is an integral part of your plan. You will talk about the key drivers of the business in the plan and about the risks. If the cash forecast shows you need more money then you must either plan to raise more money or change the plan so that you can live within your resources.